PREACHING
THE *Other* WAY

HOW TO DEVELOP **A TEACHING TEAM** IN YOUR CHURCH

JD PEARRING

EXCEL
LEADERSHIP NETWORK

In *Preaching the Other Way*, I believe JD has been able to put into words what our fellowship has been observing, but struggling to articulate and replicate. For an organization committed to reproducing, this work is an invaluable resource. Just the section on developing a culture of feedback is more than worth the price of the book. I am so thankful for this tool to help us as we continue to pursue multiplication of leaders and churches that impact the world.

Rocky Rocholl, President of the Fellowship
of Evangelical Churches

JD Pearring captures the heart of healthy Christian leadership in *Preaching the Other Way*. While many of our current models for pastoral leadership lead to burnout, personal failure, and harm to immediate family members, JD offers exceptional guidance for emotional and spiritual health for those fulfilling the call of the gospel. This book integrates biblical wisdom, years of experience, and sound psychological principles that will encourage those in pastoral ministry. Whether you are considering how to carry out God's call for your life, or have been in ministry for many years, the challenges in this book will bring freedom and renewal!

Brett Dowdy, Psy.D., Psychologist
Chief of Psychological Services, Lindner Center of HOPE

Exploring the excuses we communicators create, *Preaching the Other Way* reminds pastors that "our primary job isn't to do the work as much as it is to equip other people to do his work." In this book, practitioner and pastor JD Pearring systematically, biblically, and compellingly addresses each skeptical question as to why team teaching is imperative, what it is, who can do it, and how, where, and when. JD illustrates through scripture and example how "the biblical pattern could easily be seen as a model for team teaching. It suggests that the primary goal of leadership is multiplication, not necessarily mega-church ministry." Simultaneously refreshingly humble yet with conviction, Pearring's *Preaching the Other Way* is a healthy ego check coupled with practical, tangible, and even encouraging guidance for current and developing pastors. I am sharing this book with my pastor and recommending it to every preacher I know.

Nathan "Chivo" Hawkins
Stadia West Regional Director

Preaching the Other Way
by JD Pearring

© Copyright 2018 by James David (JD) Pearring Sr. All rights reserved.

Published in collaboration with  LAMP POST inc.
www.lamppostpublishers.com

Published by:

EXCEL LEADERSHIP PUBLISHING

8737 Santa Ridge Circle • Elk Grove • CA • 95624
www.excelleadershipnetwork.com

Trade Paperback: ISBN-13 # 978-1-60039-123-1
ebook: ISBN-13 # 978-1-60039-097-5

To Tim Pearring, Ben Finney and Jeff Sammons.
—Journey Church Teaching Team Leaders

And to Lori Pearring, Tricia Pearring Chen, Scott Pearring,
Jake Pearring, Melissa Anderson, David Bennett, Adam Burrell,
Mary Beth Burrell, Scotty Foundain, Matt Golab, Sandy Hope,
Nick Hopkins, Tres Johnson, Scott Jones, Homer Lewings,
Jonathan Lewings, Josh McCormick, Anna Osborne,
Galen Reames, and Brad Schottle.
—Journey Church Teaching Team Partners

Contents

When I first heard JD Pearring preach, it wasn't in the most conducive environment to receive the heart of his message. It was just before my wife, Farrah, and I were going to receive our results from a four-day church planter's assessment called Discovery Center. If you've never been assessed, picture *The Voice*, *Survivor*, and a dose of *American Ninja Warrior* thrown in (or that's what it felt like from an intensity standpoint at least). We were waiting for results that would potentially shape our future (think red light, yellow light, green light—and we really wanted a green light!) and we had to sit through an agonizing message from the guy who might tell you, "You are not cut out to plant a church."

From the moment JD began to speak, my attention was captured, and within minutes my heart was moved. By the way, those are critical factors in a great preacher's ability to move someone; they have to be captivating and motivating, not just educating. JD was both. I've heard him give that same message more than twenty times since joining the Discovery Center staff over ten years ago. Every time I hear it, I receive something new. I am captivated again. I am determined to grow in my own preaching as I serve the church we planted, Rivers Crossing Community Church in

Cincinnati, Ohio. JD Pearring has the credibility to write a book on preaching because he's got tenure, yes, but more so because he's an incredible preacher.

I have been preaching for more than two decades, and I've seen the Church try to do everything to attract people, often minimizing the importance of preaching in the health and growth of a local church. Some have gone as far to say that preaching is dead. Preaching is ineffective. Preaching has lost its impact on culture. Mark Twain, when he was aging and sick, famously said, "The reports of my death are greatly exaggerated." Well, I think the reports of preaching's death are greatly exaggerated. Preaching, and preaching with excellence, is one of the most powerful tools that God has given the church to reach the lost, grow disciples, and equip the saints.

In a Pew Research Center's study[1] on why people choose a church, 83% of the people say that the quality of the sermon was the most important factor in choosing a church. More than feeling welcomed. More than the style of services, kid's programs, and location. Preaching. Without a doubt the quality of your preaching matters.

JD has discovered what I believe is the missing ingredient in many pulpits: more than one ingredient! Someone needs to say it and I pray that some church boards read this and support their pastor. So many churches are dominated by one burned-out pastor who is preaching forty-eight to fifty Sunday mornings a year, not to mention

---

1   Travis Mitchell, "Choosing a New Church or House of Worship," Pew Research Center's Religion & Public Life Project, October 26, 2016, , accessed November 27, 2018, http://www.pewforum.org /2016/08/23/choosing-a-new-church-or-house-of-worship/.

Sunday nights and a mid-week Bible study. Your preaching will be *better* when you have a preaching team. A team for feedback. A team for preparation. A team to prevent burnout. A team for fresh perspective. A team to reflect the Scriptures' example.

I love what JD says: "Everyone – even preachers – need a push. Why team teaching? Teaching in a team concept gives everyone a push and helps everyone improve. If we are not on a team, we may stifle our own growth." Don't stifle your growth. Let JD push you to grow as a preacher and push you to develop a team if you don't have one.

At Rivers Crossing, we have greatly benefitted from the principles that JD shares in *Preaching the Other Way.* You will gain insight into the practical how-tos of team teaching as well as fresh ideas if you are already implementing many of these principles in your context. His chapters on the bench, women, and training time are gold. JD's wisdom is priceless, but the case studies at the end of each chapter deliver where it counts: practical application and real-world implementation. I can't wait to see this book benefit not only your preaching, but the kingdom of God. Start preaching the other way. Today.

Pastor Paul Taylor
Lead Pastor | Rivers Crossing Community Church

WHY ARE YOU PREACHING EVERY SUNDAY?

In spite of the "bad-mouthing" of preaching and preachers, no one who takes the Bible seriously should count preaching out. To the New Testament writers, preaching stands as the event through which God works.

—Haddon Robinson, *Biblical Preaching*

The work of preaching is the highest and greatest and most glorious calling to which anyone can ever be called.

—Martyn Lloyd Jones

If I had to do it all over again, I'd get help.

—George Ghegan

I hesitate to write about preaching. It is such a sensitive, emotion-filled topic. And most of us preachers feel like we're already great at it. Just about everyone considers himself or herself to be a good driver, a good kisser, and a good preacher.

A pastor was driving home from church after a Sunday when he really thought he'd hit a home run with his sermon. "How many truly great preachers do you believe are out there, honey?" he confidently asked his wife. She responded, "One less than you think, dear."

Dale Hummel from Wooddale Church in Minnesota insists it's no accident we often refer to "delivering a sermon." Hummel says that preaching is somewhat like delivering a baby – we've put a ton of time, discomfort, and hard work into it. Then Hummel adds, "And no one wants to be told they have an ugly baby!"

I didn't want to write about preaching, but one event pushed me into it.

I wasn't the speaker that day, but I was on the after-message panel – in our church we regularly employ a panel to answer questions after and about the sermon. The Q & A that morning was going fine when one inquiry rocked me. Someone had texted in this question: "What regrets do you have as a parent?"

It seemed like a simple enough issue. But something about it jolted me.

I am not a man of regrets, and I have felt that I have been a pretty good dad – actually a *really* good dad. I'd followed a simple script for success: First, I tried to stay close to our heavenly father and point my kids toward Him. Second, I married well. I out-kicked my coverage when I landed Lori, who is an amazing, loving, attentive, stupendous mom. Third, I stayed married to Lori. And fourth, I valued relationship over rules with the kids. So, I fancied myself a father without regret.

I could have been a better father, a better person, a better preacher, if I would have done some things differently.

But that day one regret hit me square in the face. I'm pretty sure I wasn't even called on to answer the regret question. They picked on someone else. But I felt the Holy Spirit convict me. This thought crashed into my brain: "I preached too much."

I was a pastor the entire time our kids were growing up and I spent almost every single Sunday preaching. I typically spoke almost fifty weekends a year, which meant I had PMS – pre-message syndrome – almost every Saturday while my kids were growing up. Saturdays sucked, and it was my fault. I cluttered up every weekend with my preoccupation with the sermon – it's not necessarily a bad thing to be concerned with teaching well. But I could have been a better father, a better person, a better preacher, if I would have done some things differently.

Let me make this confession: For several years I actually preached fifty-three times per year (every Sunday and Christmas Eve.) My typical pattern was speaking forty-eight to fifty Sundays a year. I was very careful about letting someone else "fill the pulpit." I was too careful, too controlling, and too arrogant.

I have since repented. I moved from speaking all the time to speaking forty times per year. Then I reduced my sermons to twenty-six – or less – times per year. A few years ago, I stepped down and my son became the Lead Pastor. He asked me to serve as a Teaching Team Coach. Now, I preach only about once per month, and I

Preaching less has actually been one of the best gifts I could have given to myself – and my church.

am actually paid to help other people preach. My job is to put together and serve our teaching team. No more hoarding the pulpit. Preaching less has actually been one of the best gifts I could have given to myself – and my church.

I actually discovered that when I speak less, I do a better job. As good as I thought I was at speaking, I've become more skillful by not facing the task every single Sunday.

> **As good as I thought I was at speaking, I've become more skillful by not facing the task every single Sunday.**

So, I'd like to encourage you to join me as a now-recovering pulpit hoarder. Let's give the next person a chance.

Of course, I have heard the usual excuses for not letting others speak:

- **"I'm really accomplished at preaching."** It's my gift, I've always preached just about every Sunday and it's the only model I've ever seen. The church will suffer if I'm not speaking.

- **"Preaching is my main job as the Lead Pastor."** Speaking at weekend services is my primary role. They pay me to preach.

- **"There's no one else in our church who can speak effectively."** I would love to have someone to help share the heavy load of preaching, but gifted speakers are just nowhere to be found.

- **"Other people are not trained in preaching."**
  I went to Bible School, I went to Seminary.
  We may have some potential preachers in our
  midst, but they do not know what they are
  doing. I can't risk letting them loose on our
  congregation.

- **"If we had an entire team trained for preaching, where would we find opportunities for
  everyone to speak?** I get the concept, but I
  don't think there is room for more teachers.

- **"There's someone who wants to preach but
  isn't gifted."** I can't give up the pulpit because
  poor preachers would step in and make a
  mess.

- **"Our church is just not ready for a dramatic
  change like moving to team teaching."** I
  know it makes sense, but we are not there yet.

- **"Honestly, I'm a little insecure."** I'm not sure
  how I would cope if I wasn't on stage every
  Sunday, or worse yet, if somebody else in the
  church was as good or an even better preacher
  than me.

There are numerous reasonable excuses for not moving
to a teaching team approach. But in the end, they are still
just excuses.

The Top Ten Excuses from a Closed Mind

10.   We tried that before, it didn't work.

9.   Our situation is different.

8.   It'll cost too much.

7.   We don't have the time.

6.   It's against company policy.

5.   That's not our problem.

4.   We're not ready for that.

3.   Let's form a committee.

2.   It's too much trouble to change.

1.   We've never done it that way before.

In their book, *Extreme Ownership*, Navy Seals leaders Jocko Willink and Leif Babin write: "Once people stop making excuses, stop blaming others, and take ownership of everything in their lives, they are compelled to take action to solve their problems. They are better leaders, better followers, more dependable and actively contributing team members, and more skilled in aggressively driving toward mission accomplishment. But they're also humble – able to keep their egos from damaging relationships and adversely impacting the mission and the team."[2]

> "The test of a preacher is that his congregation goes away saying, not 'What a lovely sermon,' but, 'I will do something.'"

Brian Moran insists, "You can make all the excuses you want; the world doesn't care. As harsh as that sounds, it's the truth. Oh, you may from time to time get a little sympathy,

---

2   Jocko Willink and Leif Babin, *Extreme Ownership: How U.S. Navy SEALs Lead and Win* (New York: St. Martins, 2017), Kindle Edition.

and maybe if you're really lucky a free beer, but that's about it… Resolve right now to never again let excuses get in the way of you achieving your goals."[3]

I want to encourage you to get past the excuse barriers and take a big step toward preaching the other way – with, in and through a team.

This book will seek to work through the objections to team teaching by tackling the excuses, while offering practical tips on how to form and develop a teaching team. We will primarily look at the Bible's Book of Acts for how the early church leaders tackled this topic, and we will do so in a format of: Why? What? Who? How? Where? When?

This book is aimed primarily at preachers – those who are regular speakers, who are often "in the pulpit" of their church or ministry. But it is also designed to help two other groups: 1. Those who do any Christian teaching – full-time speakers, part-time presenters; 2. Those who think they might have a gift or talent for preaching or teaching (in this book I don't go into the different definitions or nuances in preaching versus teaching) or public speaking and want to pursue growing in their gift.

All proceeds from this book will go to promote new churches starting all over the world through Excel Leadership Network and its partners – hopefully all of those new churches will employ a team teaching approach as well.

It would be silly to write a book on teaching teams solely from one man's perspective, so this is a more than

---

3   Brian Moran and Michael Lennington, *The 12 Week Year: Get More Done in 12 Weeks than Others Do in 12 Months* (Hoboken, NJ: Wiley, 2013), 146.

a solo opinion. The teaching teams at Journey Church worked through this material. And each chapter features a church that is implementing a team teaching approach. These real-life examples are from leaders who are friends of mine, colleagues, and fellow travelers on the team journey.

And each chapter will include a "Big Challenge" to help put the principles into practice.

Francis De Sales concluded, "The test of a preacher is that his congregation goes away saying, not 'What a lovely sermon,' but, 'I will do something.'"[4]

Action is not just the test of a preacher – it is also the best test of a book.

THE BIG CHALLENGE:

Using the lists of excuses in the introduction of the book as a reference, make a list of your own excuses that may be keeping you from trying a teaching team in your ministry. Pray over the list, asking the Holy Spirit to help you see which excuses are valid and what some possible solutions might be.

---

4   "Francis De Sales," *Encyclopedia Britannica*, Volume 9, 613.

PREACHING
THE *Other* WAY

PART ONE

WHY?

CHAPTER 1

GET BACK

In most business settings, presentations are team affairs.

—Peter Coughter, *The Art of the Pitch*

Make ministry a team sport, it's a lot more fun.

—Chris Brown

When a lead pastor sets up a teaching team, he sets an example for all the other leaders. It broadens the church's ministry by making more people participants and fewer people spectators. It guards against burnout in an individual. And it establishes leaders that can "seed" another church plant.

—Jeff Sammons

A professor heard about an actual dinosaur still alive in the rainforests of South America. So the professor launched a scientific expedition. After several weeks he stumbled upon a little man wearing a loincloth, standing near a 300-foot-long dead dinosaur. The scientist couldn't believe it. "Did you kill this dinosaur?" he asked. "Yep," replied the rainforest native. "But it's so big and you're so small! How did you kill it?" the professor inquired. "With my club," the primitive fellow answered. "How big is your club?" asked the scientist? The little man answered, "Well, there are about a hundred of us…"

> Now in the church at Antioch there were proph-
> ets and teachers: Barnabas, Simeon called Niger,
> Lucius of Cyrene, Manaen (who had been brought
> up with Herod the tetrarch) and Saul.
>
> Acts 13:1 (NIV)

The church in Antioch was arguably the greatest church in history.

> The disciples were called Christians first at Antioch.
>
> Acts 11:26 (NIV)

This church put Christianity on the map. And in this incredible assembly there was a teaching *team*. It wasn't a gathering with one superstar pastor, a rock star preacher, or the same teacher speaking at every meeting. There was a team.

We might think the team concept was just an anomaly for the church in Antioch, until we are reminded of the Apostle Paul's exhortation in his second letter to Timothy:

> And the things you have heard me say in the pres-
> ence of many witnesses entrust to reliable men who
> will also be qualified to teach others.
>
> 2 Timothy 2:2 (NIV)

Paul directs leaders to develop teachers.

We see this again as Paul instructs the Corinthians about their order of worship.

What then shall we say, brothers and sisters? When you come together, each of you has a hymn, or a word of instruction, a revelation, a tongue or an interpretation. Everything must be done so that the church may be built up. If anyone speaks in a tongue, two – or at the most three – should speak, one at a time, and someone must interpret. If there is no interpreter, the speaker should keep quiet in the church and speak to himself and to God.

Two or three prophets should speak, and the others should weigh carefully what is said. And if a revelation comes to someone who is sitting down, the first speaker should stop. For you can all prophesy in turn so that everyone may be instructed and encouraged.

1 Corinthians 14:26-31(NIV)

I'm not going to pretend that I understand everything or even most things about these directions. And I'm not sure that all of us have to be on the same page as to what speaking in tongues means or the exact definition of a prophet. But I do think we can get some consensus that more than one person was involved in the speaking part of the services. There appears to be a team in the early church preaching world.

There appears to be a team in the early church preaching world.

A broad look at the Book of Acts reveals these people giving some sort of sermon, message or proclamation:

Clearly, there is a lot of Peter and a lot of Paul, but there are at least twenty others who preached.

The biblical pattern could easily be seen as a model for team teaching. It suggests that the primary goal of leadership is multiplication, not necessarily mega-church ministry. The early church leaders were constantly looking to identify and develop the next tier and the next generation of leaders. Let's get back to this biblical pattern. If it was good for Paul and Silas, it should be good enough for us.

> So it makes no difference whether I preach or they preach, for we all preach the same message you have already believed.
>
> 1 Corinthians 15:11 (NLT)

Now these are the gifts Christ gave to the church: the apostles, the prophets, the evangelists, and the pastors and teachers. Their responsibility is to

equip God's people to do his work and build up the
church, the body of Christ.

Ephesians 4:11-12 (NLT)

We preachers need to be continually reminded that our
primary job isn't to do the work as much as it is to equip
other people to do his work.

Several racehorses are resting in a stable. One of them
starts to boast about his track record. "In the last sixteen
races, I've won eight of them!" Another horse breaks in,
"Well in the last twenty-seven races, I've won twenty!!"
"Oh, that's good, but in the last thirty-seven races, I've won
twenty-nine!" says another, flicking his tail. At this point,
they notice that a greyhound dog has been sitting there listening. "I don't mean to boast," says the greyhound, "but
in my last ninety-one races, I've won eighty-nine of them!"
The horses are clearly amazed. "Wow!" says one, after a
hushed silence, "A talking dog!"

What is the point of that joke? There are probably
more speaking gifts around than we ever thought.

For years I have considered the seven spiritual gifts listed
in Romans chapter 12 as the seven primary gift categories:

In his grace, God has given us different gifts for
doing certain things well. So if God has given you
the ability to prophesy, speak out with as much
faith as God has given you. If your gift is serving
others, serve them well. If you are a teacher, teach
well. If your gift is to encourage others, be encouraging. If it is giving, give generously. If God has

given you leadership ability, take the responsibility
seriously. And if you have a gift for showing kindness to others, do it gladly.

Romans 12:6-8 (NLT)

Paul lists prophet, serving, teaching, encouragement,
giving, leadership and mercy among the gifts. At least one
of these has to do with teaching, and if you count prophet
and encouragement, then three out of seven are speaking
gifts. Somewhere between 15% and 40% of gifts have
to do with speaking, and yet the typical church in North
America has one person doing over 90% of the sermons?

Jesus said, "As the Father has sent me, I am sending
you" (John 20:21, NLT).

Luke added this about the Apostle Paul, "Then he
dispatched to Macedonia two of his assistants, Timothy
and Erastus, while he himself stayed for a while in Asia"
(Acts 19:22, Phillips).

The clear biblical approach to teaching reveals it is a
team affair, and the goal is reproducing disciples, leaders
and teachers.

Sermons in the early days of the church consisted
of reading simple scripture passages, followed by a short
explanation and exhortation. The synagogue at the time of
Christ had a time of interactive discussion after a speaker
finished. Jesus most often spoke and then dialogued with
his listeners. In the early church, since most services were
held house to house (Acts 20:20), it didn't take long for
church services to be formalized with communion holding
the primary position in the meetings.

Within a couple of hundred years preaching became the sole responsibility of bishops – even Augustine and Chrysostom only preached with permission of their bishop. Historian Jeffrey T. Sammons explains:

> Increasingly Latin became the standard language of the church, and as the Roman Empire collapsed in the 300s-400s only the educated few (maybe 1%) could understand the sermons. It was not uncommon in the Middle Ages for priests to read sermons in Latin though their parishioners didn't know the language. Many priests were illiterate, and they basically faked reading scripture and sermons secure in the knowledge that their equally illiterate parishioners would never find out. As early as John Wycliffe in the 1380s, some in the Catholic Church felt the people standing in the church ought to understand the Bible and began translating it into their everyday languages. With the beginning of the Protestant Reformation in 1517, Bibles were translated and produced in languages besides Latin. The printing press also made Bibles more available, so knowledge of the Word became broadened.
>
> Protestants also believed in the priesthood of all believers while eliminating the hierarchy that had ruled the Catholic Church (bishops, cardinals and popes). Preaching then became the responsibility of the local pastor, who was expected to give a hundred different sermons each year, each about forty-five minutes long. About this time pews began

appearing in churches so people could sit during these sermons. In 1519, Swiss reformer Ulrich Zwingli announced he would no longer give the approved sermon, but would go right through the New Testament "from A to Z." Now the preaching of the Word in a language they understood became the focal point of the service, replacing communion and ritual.

Martin Luther encouraged his students to manuscript their messages, and even provided catechisms as a sort of FAQ to push the team concept, but within a generation of his death, Lutheran orthodoxy settled in, clearly stifling innovation.

During the 1700s, the Wesley Brothers in England and the First Great Awakening in America expanded preaching into the realm of the lay preacher. But after their deaths the tradition of one expert preacher again ruled the day.

And it still exists today. Larry Osborne calls this "The Holy Man Myth": "It's the idea that pastors and clergy somehow have a more direct line to God. It cripples a church because it overburdens pastors and underutilizes the gifts and anointing of everyone else. It mistakenly equates leadership gifts with superior spirituality. …I could never figure out how people's seeming dependence on my prayers, advice, and physical presence squared with our stated belief in the priesthood of the believer – the New Testament doctrine that every follower of Christ has the privilege of direct access to God. It's hardly a peripheral doctrine. It's one that God himself emphasized when he ripped open the temple curtain that had, until Jesus' death, separated the Holy of Holies from everyone but the high priest. This event symbolized the end of an era when a special holy man was needed to stand in the gap to mediate between God and man."[5]

In the last decade, there has been an encouraging push toward team ministry and an increasing momentum to get back to the biblical example of multiple teachers and the biblical directive toward multiplication.

Cathedrals, Catacombs and a Catastrophe

Recently my wife, Lori, and I went over to Europe to support a church planter there and to speak at one of the new work's services. We flew into Germany, where Lori's brother, Mike, and our sister-in-law, Pandora, live. Mike and Pandora drove us to Linz, Austria, to serve the church planter. On the trip we stopped at numerous old cathedrals and church buildings. Mike is a big fan of cathedrals. I am not. Inside one of the old structures, my wife asked, "Well, what do you think?" "This makes me so sad," I responded. The architecture communicated that God is far away and disinterested in us, and worse yet, the empty church buildings declare that we have missed the point. We've been consumed with ourselves at the expense of reproducing leaders and teachers.

> **We've been consumed with ourselves at the expense of reproducing leaders and teachers.**

---

5   Larry Osborne, *Sticky Church* (Grand Rapids, MI: Zondervan, 2008).

On the trip, Lori and I were able to sneak away for a couple of days in Paris. We were not sure which sights were must-see, but a fellow Uber rider suggested we check out the underground catacombs. "Six million people are buried there," he maintained. "There is no way six million corpses are there," I thought, so we asked to be dropped off at the catacombs and walked down the numerous flights of stairs to investigate. We wandered through hundreds and thousands and maybe even six million skeletons! Most were neatly stacked with skulls at the top and leg bones at the bottom, with the rest of the remains in between.

It was a mortifying experience. There actually could be six million or more bodies buried there. I tried not to touch anything and quickly washed my hands as we went to leave the site. When we stepped outside, I noticed something we'd never see in the United States: apartment complex after apartment complex built right on top of the catacombs. Thousands of people lived above the burial ground property.

Life is short. We all are standing on the shoulders of those who came before us. Thoughts of mortality engulfed me. But it wasn't my own transience that struck me, or even my kids' mortality. I reflected on my grandkids. Do the math – if there are 330 million people in America today, in a hundred years probably at least 300 million of us will be dead. Where will we bury the bodies? More importantly than that, who will be carrying on after us? Who will be preaching in a hundred years? Will it be preachers and teachers who were trained by people I trained, or will my messages die with me?

From Paris we took a train and met Mike and Pandora in the town of Metz, France. In late June of 1944, my father was dropped in the shallow waters off the coast of Normandy. He and his fellow soldiers marched across France, liberating it from German occupation. On November 9, 1944, as he walked up a hill in Metz, my Dad was hit by a bomb. He was messed up pretty badly; he spent months in a hospital, he lost his left eye, and he ended up with some awesome scars that terrified his kids. When I was a boy, about once every year or so Dad would have a doctor remove some piece of shrapnel that worked its way to the top of his skin.

Will we leave empty cathedrals and unfulfilled hopes as our legacy?

My brother-in-law Mike is a military veteran, and he had managed to track down some combat plans for that "Battle of Metz" in November of 1944. We drove around Metz looking for the actual hill where my Dad was hit. It was a surreal experience.

Dad didn't talk about his war experience much. But one time he did open up. Holding his thumb and forefinger about an inch apart, Dad smiled and revealed, "You know son, a piece of shrapnel came about this close to my, you know...private parts. So, you were this close to never being born." That statement flooded my thoughts as we drove through the hills of Metz.

Honestly, all of us were "this close" to never being born. But God sovereignly and strategically has us on this earth for our short time. Will we leave empty cathedrals and unfulfilled hopes as our legacy? Or will we teach about

Jesus in a way that trains and empowers others to keep the message going?

Let's get back to the biblical mandate and find reliable people to train so they can teach others also.

MINI CASE STUDY:
NORTH COAST CHURCH, VISTA, CALIFORNIA

Larry Osborne was one of the first pastors in our generation to embrace a teaching team approach. He started doing so when North Coast was just a few hundred in attendance and most often preached no more than twenty-five to thirty-two times a year. Today, Chris Brown, Christopher Hilken, and Larry share the teaching load at North Coast, with Larry speaking only about eighteen to twenty times a year.

He brought nationally-known speaker Chris Brown on to the staff at North Coast and eventually gave Chris a big chunk of the preaching opportunities. Now they both serve as Lead Pastors.

Presently, Larry speaks about twenty-two weekends per year, Chris speaks about twenty-two times per year, and an emerging team, which meets weekly, handles the other weekends.

Each week, the team opens up their sermon-prep message meeting to anyone in the church. It isn't collaboration, it is research. Whoever is speaking that weekend shares where they are going, and the group offers suggestions, insight, and input. But the speaker has veto-power. They can take the advice or leave it.

Osborne cites three upsides to a teaching team approach:

1. *It makes for a healthy pastor.*

Ministry is a grind, but with a team approach, "The pastor can actually have a life." Sharing the load allows a pastor to work on leadership and it keeps the sermons fresh.

2. *It makes for a healthy pastor's family.*

Osborne says that when a pastor's kids reach first grade, "it messes with the family." Having a team lessens this burden. "Spouses and kids love the weekends when the pastor doesn't have to preach." They can attend the church services like everyone else and gain a new, more accurate perspective.

3. *It makes for a healthy church.*

The church hears different voices and passions and is not so dependent on one person.

THE BIG CHALLENGE:

After reading about the church at Antioch and the case study of Larry Osborne's North Coast Church, make a list of potential benefits that a teaching team would provide your particular ministry, especially in the areas of present and future growth. *Bonus: Compare this list to the list of excuses that you made from the introduction. Which carries more weight?*

CHAPTER 2

TEAMWORK MAKES THE SCHEME WORK

Experience is indeed a teacher, but only as a member of a larger faculty.

—Fred B. Craddock, *Preaching*

Talent wins games, but teamwork wins championships.

—Michael Jordan

We don't accomplish anything in this world alone ... and whatever happens is the result of the whole tapestry of one's life and all the weavings of individual threads from one to another that creates something.

—Sandra Day O'Connor

I am writing this on the day Haddon Robinson died. Dr. Robinson was the president of Denver Seminary when I attended there. His classic book, *Biblical Preaching*, might be the best preaching book ever written. It was the text for our preaching classes. We never skipped out when Robinson spoke at chapels or special events. I regularly invited him to speak at the church I was serving, and I went out of my way to hear him preach. Every year, Robinson would choose ten to twelve seniors to attend an advanced preaching course he taught. Robinson insisted it wasn't actually a class. He called it, "Discipleship, with preaching as the main topic."

I learned more about preaching from that class than any other experience in ministry. But the bulk of the learning didn't come from instruction or presentations – it was the discussion afterward that made the most impact. The personal tips from Haddon Robinson, the push back, the questioning, "Why did you word it that way?" and his insistence on not bringing notes into the pulpit influence me to this day. "If you are prepared and then forget some part of your message," he would say, "it means that part didn't fit."

We just might learn best in a collaborative setting, when we are part of a team.

I remember talking with Scott Wenig – then a classmate, now a preaching instructor – in the seminary library after one of Robinson's senior sessions with us. We had an "aha" moment when we realized Robinson was saying that creating tension is a huge key to sermonizing.

We just might learn best in a collaborative setting, when we are part of a team, or when we are in a cohort.

Stu Streeter claims, "Communal eats individual for breakfast."

Cohorts existed in the New Testament:

> Meanwhile, a Jew named Apollos, an eloquent speaker who knew the Scriptures well, had arrived in Ephesus from Alexandria in Egypt. He had been taught the way of the Lord, and he taught others about Jesus with an enthusiastic spirit and with accuracy. However, he knew only about John's baptism. When Priscilla and Aquila heard him preaching

boldly in the synagogue, they took him aside and explained the way of God even more accurately.

Acts 18:24-26 (NLT)

Apollos was enthusiastic and even truthful, but he became a better, more precise communicator through teaming up with Priscilla and Aquilla.

Mohammed Ali was flying on a jet one day while he was Heavyweight Title champion. The flight attendant asked him to buckle up his seat belt. He said, "Superman don't need no seat belt." The flight attendant replied, "Superman don't need no airplane!" He buckled up.

If we think we're all we need, we're setting ourselves up for a crash.

In her best-selling book, *Grit*, Angela Duckworth tells about Dan Chambliss, a sociologist who spent years studying expert swimmers. He concluded about what makes a great athlete:

> "…the most important thing," Dan said. "The real way to become a great swimmer is to join a great team."
>
> That logic might strike you as strange. You might assume that *first* a person becomes a great swimmer and *then* he or she joins a great team. And it's true, of course, that great teams don't take just anyone. There are tryouts. There are a limited number of spots. There are standards. And the more elite the team, the fiercer the desire of those already on the team to keep those standards high.

What Dan was getting at is the reciprocal effect of a team's particular culture on the person who joins it. In his many years in and out of the pool, he'd seen the arrow of causality between a great team and a great individual performer go both ways. In effect, he'd witnessed the corresponsive principle of personality development: he'd seen that the very characteristics that are selected for certain situations are, in turn, enhanced by them.

"Look, when I started studying Olympians, I thought, 'What kind of oddball gets up every day at four in the morning to go to swimming practice? These must be extraordinary people to do that sort of thing.' But the thing is, when you go to a place where basically *everybody* you know is getting up at four in the morning to go to practice, that's just what you do. It's no big deal. It becomes a habit."

Over and over, Dan had observed new swimmers join a team that did things a notch or two better than what they'd been used to. Very quickly, the newcomer conformed to the team's norms and standards.

"Speaking for myself," Dan added, "I don't have that much self-discipline. But if I'm surrounded by people who are writing articles and giving lectures and working hard, I tend to fall in line. If I'm in a crowd of people doing things a certain way, I follow along."[6]

---

6   Angela Duckworth, *Grit: The Power of Passion and Perseverance* (New York, NY: Scribner, 2018), Kindle Edition, 246-247.

Super Bowl-winning coach Tony Dungy tells a similar story:

> In the 2008 Summer Olympic Games in Beijing, China, Michael Phelps was aiming to win eight events. If successful, he would break American swimmer Mark Spitz's 1972 record of seven gold medals in a single Olympic Games. To accomplish the feat, Phelps needed to win the 4x100 meter freestyle relay, which consists of four swimmers from each competing country's team each swimming one hundred meters of the freestyle, or two lengths of the pool, down and back.
>
> The US team was well behind after the third leg, when Jason Lezak dived into the pool. No one watching in the crowd or glued to their televisions gave him any chance of overtaking France's Alain Bernard on the final anchor leg of the relay. It looked as though the United States would again lose this relay race – a race they had captured gold in seven times before – for the third straight summer games. But the crowd and the millions watching weren't swimming that final lap, and they hadn't consulted one key person: Jason Lezak.
>
> At thirty-two, Jason was the oldest swimmer on the US team. He started the final leg well back of Bernard – the reigning world record holder in the 100-meter freestyle – and at the final turn, he was still a full body length behind. He had many opportunities along the way to concede and accept

second place; everyone else had already assumed he couldn't overtake Bernard's enormous lead. But there was no quit in Lezak, and with one incredible last stroke he bested the world's best to win the relay for the United States by a fingertip and set a new world record. And Michael Phelps, with the help of his teammates, went on to achieve his goal.

As I recall hearing in an interview with Lezak after the race, he didn't think he would have caught Bernard in an individual race – the deficit was too big. However, because it was a relay, Lezak felt he was swimming for his teammates, so he couldn't just give up.

We need to feel that same way – we're doing what we're doing for the Lord, so we can't just give up.[7]

Olympic and World Cup soccer champion Mia Hamm wrote in her book, *Go for the Goal*, "Soccer is not an individual sport. I don't score all the goals, and the ones I do score are usually the product of a team effort. I don't keep the ball out of the back of the net on the other side of the field. I don't plan our game tactics. I

Growth through teamwork is one of the keys to effectiveness.

don't wash the training gear (okay, sometimes I do), and I don't make our airline reservations. I am a member of a team, and I rely on the team. I defer to it and sacrifice

---

7   Tony Dungy and Nathan Whitaker, *The One Year Uncommon Life Daily Challenge* (Carol Stream, IL: Tyndale House Publishers, 2011), Kindle Edition, Locations 5011-5015.

for it, because the team, not the individual, is the ultimate champion."[8]

Growth through teamwork is one of the keys to effectiveness, and not just in the world of sports. In *Extreme Ownership*, Jocko Willink and Leif Babin talk about teamwork in combat and beyond:

> Among the legions of leadership books in publication, we found most focus on individual practices and personal character traits. We also observed that many corporate leadership training programs and management consulting firms do the same. But without a team – a group of individuals working to accomplish a mission – there can be no leadership. The only meaningful measure for a leader is whether the team succeeds or fails. For all the definitions, descriptions, and characterizations of leaders, there are only two that matter: effective and ineffective. Effective leaders lead successful teams that accomplish their mission and win. Ineffective leaders do not.[9]

Dr. Franklin Murphy excelled in a variety of fields – he was a great doctor, the dean of the University of Kansas Medical School, Chancellor of UCLA, and Chairman of the Times-Mirror Corporation. He attributed his success to this secret, "The people around me have made me

---

8   Mia Hamm and Aaron Heifetz, *Go for the Goal: A Champions Guide to Winning in Soccer and Life* (New York: Quill, 2002).

9   Willink and Babin, *Extreme Ownership*, 8.

successful. I would never have been able to accomplish anything on my own. I have always sought out people who I felt were talented, who had self-discipline. I have tried to develop their affection and loyalty. I have recruited them, motivated them, and when we were able to achieve something, I shared the credit with them."[10]

Brian Merchant, author of *The One Device: The Secret History of the iPhone*, reveals that Steve Jobs didn't really invent the iPhone. It was a team effort. The vast majority of inventions came out of team effort:

> We now know, for instance, that Edison most certainly did not invent the lightbulb – he simply perfected it as a consumer product. His team found the ideal bamboo filament that made his bulb's glow much more appealing than the competition. And even then, Edison manned a large lab staffed by brilliant researchers...So it is with Steve Jobs and the iPhone... What Jobs did at Apple with the iPhone was take a smattering of percolating technologies and drove his team to integrate them in a way never executed so elegantly before. The key word is "team."
>
> The thing that concerns me about the Steve Jobs and Edison complex is that young people who are being trained as innovators or designers are being sold the Edison myth, the genius designer, the great innovator, the Steve Jobs, the Bill Gates,

---

10   Jack Canfield and Janet Switzer, *The Success Principles: How to Get from Where You Are to Where You Want to Be* (New York: William Morrow, 2015).

or whatever. They're never being taught the notion of the collective, the team, the history.[11]

Teamwork pushes everyone to be better.

A couple is in bed sleeping when there's a *rat-a-tat-tat* on the door. The husband rolls over and looks at the clock, and its half past three in the morning. "I'm not getting out of bed at this time," he thinks, and rolls over. Then a louder knock follows. So he drags himself out of bed, goes downstairs, opens the door, and there's a man standing there. It didn't take the homeowner long to realize the man was drunk.

> **Teamwork pushes everyone to be better.**

"Hi there," slurs the stranger. "Can you give me a push?" "No, get lost. It's half past three and I was in bed," says the man as he slams the door. He goes back up to bed and tell his wife what happened, and she says, "That wasn't very nice of you. Remember that night we broke down in the pouring rain on the way to pick the kids up from the baby-sitter and you had to knock on that man's house to get us started again? What would have happened if he'd told us to get lost?" "But the guy was drunk," says the husband. "It doesn't matter," says the wife." He needs our help and it would be the Christian thing to help him." So the husband gets out of bed again, gets dressed, and goes downstairs. He opens the door, and not being able to see the stranger anywhere, he shouts, "Hey, do you still want a push?" And he hears a voice cry out, "Yeah, please." So,

---

11 Brian Merchant, "Steve Jobs Did Not Invent the iPhone," *LinkedIn* (blog), July 1, 2017.

still being unable to see the stranger he shouts, "Where are you?" The drunk replies, "Over here, on the swing."

Everyone – even preachers – need a push.

Why team teaching? Teaching in a team concept gives everyone a push and helps everyone improve.

If we are not on a team, we may stifle our own growth.

In her work entitled *The Derailment of Fast-Track Managers*, Rutgers professor Barbara Roach says, "Many so-called whiz-kids fizzle because they fail to share power with others. In the early years of their career they are individualistic and achievement oriented, focusing on what they themselves can accomplish through their own efforts. Much of this must be forgotten in the mid-years of their careers when the transition from individual to group achievement, from solo flights to partnership, and from competition to cooperation must be learned. Then in the senior years one must create an environment in which many others can achieve, and where the measure of one's work is, in fact, the measure of the work of others."[12]

> **Teaching in a team concept gives everyone a push and helps everyone improve.**

Have you ever wondered why geese fly in a V-formation? They can fly farther in that formation because it creates an updraft, and they don't get as tired when they fly together. And when we fly, when we walk, when we run through life together, we're a whole lot less tired.

Lefty Gomez still holds a marvelous pitching record in the World Series. He won six games and didn't lose any in

---

12 Barbara Roach, "The Derailment of Fast-Track Managers."

his World Series performances. Once when asked what his secret of success was, Gomez answered, "Clean living and a fast outfield." No one succeeds by himself.

The Gospel Herald touts a sure-fire formula for success: "Surround yourself with people who are smarter than you are."

Goethe was on to it when he wrote, "The greatest genius will not be worth much if he pretends to draw exclusively from his own resources."

If we are to truly be effective in life, we need to connect with a team. If we're to truly be effective teachers and preachers, teamwork is a must.

MINI CASE STUDY:
COMUNIDAD CRISTIANA, EL NIÑO, MEXICO

Pastor Tury Nunez on working with a Teaching Team: "I love it; it brings a different perspective to the church when we can craft and work on the series and messages together."

Pastor Tury utilizes a team of four preachers who each speak about twelve times on an annual basis. The speakers tend to keep a regular rotation, so each preaches about once per month.

The speakers have been selected through relationships that have been deepened over a number of years. Tury's father, Daniel, was the former pastor of the church. He started the teaching team approach, and it led to a smooth hand-off to his son.

The mantra of the team is, "Everybody on the same page and no surprises on stage."

The team meets regularly to primarily pray for the messages and to talk through them. The team plans out series well in advance and they are relentless about giving healthy feedback to each other.

Intentionality in spending time with and developing team members is a key part of the team, since most of the regular preachers are unpaid volunteers.

THE BIG CHALLENGE:

Examine your ministry's current teaching protocol. Brainstorm some ideas of how to introduce more opportunities for feedback and collaboration from others. Continue this process at your next church leadership meeting. Focus on the goal of increasing the quality and depth of the teaching at your church by getting more people involved.

CHAPTER 3

THE THIRD KEY

I try to take one day at a time, but sometimes several days attack me at once.

—Ashleigh Brilliant

There is no decision that we can make that doesn't come with some sort of balance or sacrifice.

—Simon Sinek

It marks a big step in your development when you come to realize that other people can help you do a better job than you could do alone.

—Andrew Carnegie

Last Friday my friend Jimmy was in our garage working on my 1966 Ford Mustang Convertible. Jimmy is the only one I let work on my classic ragtop. And Jimmy doesn't even let *me* work on that vehicle since my mechanical skills hover somewhere between challenged and non-existent. I asked Jimmy if I could do anything to help. When he said, "Yes," I was excited and nervous. He approached me, took out a wad of keys from his pocket, identified one in particular and handed the entire ring to me by that key. "This is the key to my house," he said. "Go inside through the house to my garage and grab two jack stands. That will be a big help."

Running errands to pick up stuff is a good fit for my car-fixing abilities, so I headed out. Ever the multitasker, I figured I could do some leadership recruiting on the phone while accomplishing operation, "Get Jack Stands!" So, I was engrossed in a recruiting conversation when I pulled on to Jimmy's street. With headphones on I approached the front door and put Jimmy's key into the front door. It didn't fit. I tried the key in the dead bolt, it didn't work there either. I tried both again, all while continuing my phone dialogue. The key still didn't match.

Just as I was dreading the thought of having to try every single key on the enormous ring, the door opened from the inside. A thirty-something girl stood behind the door. I didn't recognize her. What's worse, she didn't recognize me. She started screaming in a language I couldn't identify. As I backed away, she opened the screen door and continued shrieking as she charged toward me. I didn't know what else to do besides shouting, "Jimmy? Jimmy? Is this Jimmy's place?" My phone buddy asked what was happening. I ran toward my car, hopped in, and raced down the street, where I soon discovered Jimmy's actual house.

It is important to have the right key *and* the right house.

Many of us in ministry are disappointed because we haven't found the right keys. We may even feel like we're trying to open the wrong doors.

What is the key to effective ministry?

A look at the life and times of the Apostle Paul gives us some insight.

In Acts chapter 20, Paul calls for a meeting of the Ephesian elders. It is the last meeting with them that he will ever have. Paul begins the meeting by recalling his work:

> When they arrived he declared, "You know that from the day I set foot in the province of Asia until now I have done the Lord's work humbly and with many tears. I have endured the trials that came to me from the plots of the Jews...And now I am bound by the Spirit to go to Jerusalem. I don't know what awaits me, except that the Holy Spirit tells me in city after city that jail and suffering lie ahead. But my life is worth nothing to me unless I use it for finishing the work assigned me by the Lord Jesus – the work of telling others the Good News about the wonderful grace of God.
>
> Acts 20:18-24 (NLT)

Paul speaks of his amazing sacrifice. We see this theme again in the next chapter:

> Several days later a man named Agabus, who also had the gift of prophecy, arrived from Judea. He came over, took Paul's belt, and bound his own feet and hands with it. Then he said, "The Holy Spirit declares, 'So shall the owner of this belt be bound by the Jewish leaders in Jerusalem and turned over to the Gentiles.'" When we heard this, we and the local believers all begged Paul not to go on to Jerusalem. But he said, "Why all this weeping? You are breaking my heart! I am ready not only to be

jailed at Jerusalem but even to die for the sake of
the Lord Jesus."

Acts 21:10-14 (NLT)

Evidently, Paul's secret to effectiveness in ministry is
sacrifice. Unselfishness is key.

Billy Graham claimed, "The highest form of worship
is the worship of unselfish Christian service. The greatest
form of praise is the sound of consecrated feet seeking out
the lost and helpless."

Sacrifice is extremely necessary. It is one of the keys to
effective ministry. I say, one of the keys, because sacrifice
by itself isn't enough. Living a purely sacrificial life can be
like having the right key, but the wrong keyhole. Sacrifice
is great as far as it goes, it just doesn't go very far.

Selfless sacrifice leads to effectiveness, but it can also
lead to burnout, abuse, and even death.

In Winston Churchill's *Memoirs of The Second World
War*, he reported on the Unexploded Bomb squads, also
known as UXB squads. During
the war, the Nazis dropped large
numbers of delayed-action explosives on England. These bombs
weren't meant to detonate on
contact, they were designed to
land and serve as a kind of land mine – to cause uncer-
tainty and paralyze action. The bombs had to be dug up
and exploded, or defused.

> **Selfless sacrifice leads
> to effectiveness, but it
> can also lead to burnout,
> abuse, and even death.**

That's where the UXB squads came in. They were volunteers in the various cities, towns, and districts who took

this dangerous job upon themselves. Churchill said, "Some survived…Others ran twenty, thirty, or even forty courses before they met their fate."[13]

He tells of one team that consisted of "the Earl of Suffolk, his lady private secretary, and his rather aged chauffeur. They called themselves 'the Holy Trinity.'" They tackled thirty-four bombs effectively, "with urbane and smiling efficiency," Churchill wrote. But the thirty-fifth took their lives.

The problem with sacrifice is we only have so much to sacrifice.

Sacrifice is only one side of the coin, one side of the story, one side of the record. There is a flipside:

> I know that none of you among whom I have gone about proclaiming the kingdom will see my face again. Therefore I testify to you this day that I am innocent of the blood of all, for I did not shrink from declaring to you the whole counsel of God…
>
> Acts 20:25-26 (ESV)

To the elders in Ephesus, these are Paul's famous last words.

Famous last words are especially memorable. General John Sedgewick was the highest-ranking Union officer killed during the Civil War. As Confederate sharpshoot-ers sent bullets whizzing past, he sat high upon his horse, laughing at his men as they dodged about from side to side.

---

13   Winston Churchill, *The Second World War* (New York: Time, 1960).

He teased, "What will you do when they open fire along the whole line? I am ashamed of you. They couldn't hit an elephant at this dist—."

I considered the late Wayman Tisdale, the former Sacramento Kings basketball player and smooth jazz bass guitarist a friend. I will never forget his last words to me: "Call me if you need me." When my Dad passed away, his last words to me were, "Thanks for everything." Those last words are so special to me I use those phrases as often as I can these days.

Look at Paul's famous last words to these people:

> Take care and be on guard for yourselves
> Acts 20:28 (AMP)

> Pay careful attention to yourselves...
> Acts 20:25-28 (ESV)

The Apostle's famous last words and primary message for these folks consisted of: take care of yourselves. The second key to ministry effectiveness is self-care.

Wait a minute, isn't this the same Paul they begged not to go to Jerusalem because he was putting himself in harm's way? Isn't he the same guy who responded with, "You're breaking my heart."? Isn't he the one who said, "To live is Christ, to die is gain"? (Philippians 1:21, NLT)

Isn't this the very same person who touted sacrifice as crucial? What does the Apostle Paul know about taking care of himself?

Let's look. In chapter 22, Paul was about to be tortured:

As they stretched him out to flog him, Paul said to
the centurion standing there, "Is it legal for you to
flog a Roman citizen who hasn't even been found
guilty?"

Acts 22:25 (NIV)

Paul was ready to sacrifice everything, but he didn't
allow this flogging to happen without trying to take care
of himself.

A bit later Paul is in a similar predicament:

At this the high priest Ananias ordered those standing near Paul to strike him on the mouth. Then
Paul said to him, "God will strike you, you whitewashed wall! You sit there to judge me according to
the law, yet you yourself violate the law…"

Acts 23:1-3 (NIV)

Again, Paul is about to be struck, but he pushes back,
he takes care of himself.

A few verses later Paul is the target of an assassination
attempt. His nephew hears about the scheme and Paul
urges this relative to do what he can to stop the insanity. So
the nephew contacts the commander and tells him:

"Some Jews have agreed to ask you to bring Paul
before the Sanhedrin tomorrow on the pretext of
wanting more accurate information about him.
Don't give in to them…

Acts 23:12-21(NIV)

Paul was a man who constantly sacrificed, but he balanced it out by taking care of himself. Self-care is not selfish. Chris Brown calls this, "Divine selfishness – the art of protecting yourself."

Let me pause to say that these stories in the Book of Acts actually give us some clear instructions on how to deal with potentially abusive situations:

1. See the problem

Paul recognized that flogging, punching, and murder attempts are not appropriate behavior.

Too often we are so caught up in sacrificing ourselves we don't even recognize the abuse that we are facing.

When I was about ten or twelve I was the recipient in an abusive incident in my family. My older brother, John, saw this happen, so he stepped in and stopped it before it got more out of hand. That episode always bothered my brother. He would bring it up from time to time, while I didn't remember it or even thought I deserved it. It was only recently that I stopped to think it through and realized, "Wait a minute! That behavior is never acceptable; it was completely inappropriate and my problem was not seeing the problem."

> **Too often, we end up in abusive situations at church or in ministry and we don't recognize how inappropriate the behavior is.**

Too often, we end up in abusive situations at church or in ministry – like feeling guilty if we don't preach every single Sunday – and we don't recognize how inappropriate the behavior is.

2. Speak up

Paul spoke up in question form, *"Is it lawful…"* Paul spoke up in confrontational form, *"You whitewashed wall…"* (I guess this is an appropriate label to use on people, after all, it is biblical!) Paul urged his nephew to speak up. And Paul's nephew spoke up in robust form, *"Don't let them do it."*

There's an old story about a Mexican bandit who robbed a Texas bank of $250,000 and escaped across the border. A month went by and the bandit thought he was safe. He was celebrating his good fortune at a local cantina when a Texas Ranger walked up and dragged him into the dusty street. Realizing he had a communication problem, the ranger poked his head back into the bar and yelled, "Anyone in here speak English?" "I do, señor," came the reply. "Come here," the ranger said to the man who quickly became the ranger's translator. "Did he rob the bank?" the ranger asked. "He did," the translator said. "Does he still have the $250,000?" "Yes," again. The ranger pulled out his Colt 45. He held the barrel of the gun to the bandit's head and cocked the trigger. "Make sure he understands this question real good," the ranger told the translator. "Where's the money?" The frightened bandit blurted out in Spanish that the money was carefully hidden in a waterproof bag at the bottom of the well in the town plaza. The translator looked up at the ranger, paused a moment and concluded, "He says he's not afraid to die."

Sometimes our inability to communicate makes our situation worse.

Rick Warren says, "There's another word for keeping the peace, it is called, 'co-dependency.' And God wants more for us than that."

3. Set proper boundaries

All three of these situations called for clear boundaries: There will be no flogging, no striking, and no murdering.

We have to enforce limits as we take care of ourselves. Henri Nouwen wrote this about boundaries:

> "You must decide for yourself to whom and when you give access to your interior life. For years, you have permitted others to walk in and out of your life according to their needs and desires. Thus you were no longer master in your own house, and you felt increasingly used. So, too, you quickly became tired, irritated, angry and resentful. Think of a medieval castle surrounded by a moat. The drawbridge is the only access to the interior of the castle. The lord of the castle must have the power to decide when to draw the bridge and when to let it down. Without such power, he can become the victim of enemies, strangers, and wanderers. He will never feel at peace in his own castle. It is important for you to control your own drawbridge. There must be times when you keep your bridge drawn and have the opportunity to be alone, or with those to whom you feel close. Never allow yourself to become public property where anyone can walk in and out at will. You might think you

are being generous to anyone who wants to enter or leave, but you will soon find yourself losing your soul.

When you claim for yourself the power over your drawbridge, you will discover new joy and peace in your heart and find yourself able to share that joy and peace with others." [14]

4. Seek to continually forgive

We don't see any lingering effects of these incidents on Paul. He didn't paint himself as a victim. He didn't constantly identify as the object of abuse. He dealt with it, and then moved on.

"Forgiveness is God's invention for coming to terms with a world in which, despite their best intentions, people are unfair to each other and hurt each other deeply. He began by forgiving us. And he invites us all to forgive each other." [15]

> **We have to walk that delicate balance of giving it all, while watching out for ourselves.**

Paul's life illustrates the need for both keys of sacrifice and self-care. We need those two dynamics working together in our lives if we will be effective in life, and in ministry. We have to walk that delicate balance of giving it all, while watching out for ourselves. We have to maneuver the tightrope of putting our lives on the line and taking care of the one life we have.

---

14 Henri J. M. Nouwen, *The Inner Voice of Love: A Journey through Anguish to Freedom* (New York: Image Books, 1998).

15 Lewis B. Smedes, *Forgive and Forget: Healing the Hurts We Don't Deserve* (New York: HarperOne, 2007).

So how do we stay in balance?

As we look at these episodes in the story of the Apostle Paul, do you see the third key to balance? Do you see what kept Paul in balance with sacrifice and self-care?

The third key is: *Other people.*

In Acts chapter 20, it was the Ephesian elders that pulled Paul back from overdosing on sacrifice. And it was Paul who kept the Ephesians elders in balance by warning them from going too far. In chapter 21 of Acts it was Agabus the prophet, and before him Phillip the evangelist and Phillip's daughters and the local believers who urged Paul not to step over the line. Then it was the Roman commander who stepped in and kept Paul from being mobbed. In Acts 22 it was that same Roman commander who inserted himself into the situation to take care of Paul. It was that commander again in Acts 23 who kept Paul safe. Then it was Paul's nephew who took a risk to save Paul, and the commander again rescued Paul from the attempt on his life.

How did Paul maintain balance during all sorts of trials, attempted abuse, arrests, and shipwrecks?

One of the telling verses of the New Testament is the first verse in Acts 28:

> Once *we* were safe on shore, *we* learned that *we* were on the island of Malta.
>
> Acts 28:1 (NLT)

This key is we. Paul consistently had other people in his life to share the load, share the preaching, and share the guard duties to make sure he was – and they were – in balance.

David Cooke emphatically states, "We can't do this by ourselves!"

Willie Nolte adds, "It never occurred to the early Christian believers to fulfill their ministry all by themselves."

A man was hitchhiking across the United States when he was picked up by an old farmer. The farmer took out a jug of moonshine and offered it to the hitchhiker, who declined, saying he didn't drink much. "Nonsense," the farmer said, "You gotta try some." He handed the jug to the hitchhiker and said, "Take a drink." "No, thanks," the man said. "I really don't want any." But the farmer wasn't going to take no for an answer. He pulled his truck to a stop, grabbed his shotgun from behind the seat, pointed it at the traveler and repeated, "I said, take a drink." "Okay, okay," the young man said. He took a large gulp and immediately realized how powerful the stuff was. His throat muscles tightened, his eyes watered, and he started choking. "Good stuff, ain't it?" the farmer asked. "I guess so," the young man gasped. Then the farmer handed his shotgun to the hitchhiker and said, "Now you hold the gun on me and make me take a drink!"

> **It never occurred to the early Christian believers to fulfill their ministry all by themselves.**

Teamwork keeps us in balance. It helps us take care of ourselves as we take care of others.

MINI CASE STUDY:
THE BRIDGE CHURCH, FLINT, MICHIGAN

Pastor Steve Bentley describes why he uses a team approach: "Especially as a founding pastor, I don't want people to be tied to me – multiple speakers helps prevent that. Different flavors of speaking helps reach more people, and multiple speakers helps teach the people to focus on the message rather than a particular messenger."

Bentley currently has three regulars on the teaching team. They have had as many as four. He admits, "The Bridge went through a time of insecurity, and in that time, we went back to one preacher for a while. But then we moved back into a team approach."

Each team member can preach an entire series, but most often there is a rotation, with each speaker giving the message that fits best for them. The Bridge offers multiple services, so often the same weekend message will feature different messengers.

Willingness is a big value for The Bridge. Bentley will ask prospective teachers to lead the announcements or prayers on stage first. Their first ten messages are built together with the team. Beginners get a lot of help and hand holding from development to presentation.

After training and feedback – everyone gets reviewed and critiqued and praised – the teachers are given more leeway.

Pastor Steve admits that The Bridge is still in process of making the team approach work, but they are also highly committed to it. Bentley has instituted plans to hand-off the church to one of the other teachers, while he goes to start another church on the other side of Flint.

THE BIG CHALLENGE:

Ask 3 (or more) people, whose opinions you can trust to be honest and helpful, to rate you on how well you are balancing sacrifice vs. self-care. How can involving other people help to fill in any trouble areas? Use the four steps outlined in this section - see the problem, speak up, set proper boundaries, seek to continually forgive - as a guide.

CHAPTER 4

HOGGING THE GLORY

*Whoever devotes themselves to themselves will have
nothing but themselves to show for themselves."*

—Andy Stanley

*If I had only one sermon to preach it would be a sermon
against pride.*

—G. K. Chesterton

*What makes the temptation of power so seemingly
irresistible? Maybe it is that power offers an easy
substitute for the hard task of love. It seems easier to be
God than to love God, easier to control people than to
love people, easier to own life than to love life.*

—Henri Nouwen

Munchausen by Proxy Syndrome (MBPS) is a deadly disorder, where an authority figure – usually a parent, and usually the mother – intentionally causes illness in a child. The disorder was named after Baron von Munchausen, an 18th-century German dignitary known for making up stories about his experiences in order to get attention. MBPS often manifests as a child only becomes sick when he or she is in proximity of his or her mother. The mother then receives special attention from the doctor and from others who laud the mother for her sacrificial care-giving, when the mother is actually causing the child to become and remain sick. The entire disorder centers on a mother's dysfunctional need for attention.

Brian Sanders suggests that the North American Church is afflicted with Munchausen disease. Many leaders are so consumed with a need for attention they are causing and keeping churches and parishioners to become overly dependent on them.

> **Many leaders are so consumed with a need for attention they are causing and keeping churches and parishioners to become overly dependent on them.**

How do we keep this over-dependence from permeating our ministries?

Larry Walkemeyer has helped start seventeen churches out of his ministry in Long Beach, California. He says, "You can't multiply and make it about yourself."

Jesus said, "God blesses those who are humble, for they will inherit the whole earth" (Matthew 5:5, NLT).

What is the secret to living in humility?

A gushy reporter told Jack Nicklaus, "You are spectacular! Your name is synonymous with the game of golf. You really know your way around the course. What's your secret?"

Nicklaus replied, "The holes are numbered."

Lamar Sleigh's dad was a pastor in a little town and he was a pretty prominent fellow. Lamar, as a little boy, used to go around and say, "I'm Pastor Sleigh's son!" His mom thought that was kind of cocky and snobbish so she said, "Don't tell people you're Pastor Sleigh's son. Just say 'I'm

Lamar Sleigh.'" A few days later a guy asked Lamar, "Aren't you Pastor Sleigh's son?" Lamar said, "I thought I was, but mom says I'm not."

How do we battle the celebrity syndrome?

While they were at Lystra, Paul and Barnabas came upon a man with crippled feet. He had been that way from birth, so he had never walked. He was sitting and listening as Paul preached. Looking straight at him, Paul realized he had faith to be healed. So Paul called to him in a loud voice, "Stand up!" And the man jumped to his feet and started walking.

When the crowd saw what Paul had done, they shouted in their local dialect, "These men are gods in human form!" They decided that Barnabas was the Greek god Zeus and that Paul was Hermes, since he was the chief speaker. Now the temple of Zeus was located just outside the town. So the priest of the temple and the crowd brought bulls and wreaths of flowers to the town gates, and they prepared to offer sacrifices to the apostles.

But when the apostles Barnabas and Paul heard what was happening, they tore their clothing in dismay and ran out among the people, shouting, "Friends, why are you doing this? We are merely human beings – just like you! We have come to bring you the Good News that you should turn from these worthless things and turn to the living God, who made heaven and earth, the sea, and everything in them. In the past he permitted all the nations to go their own ways, but he never left them without evidence of himself and his goodness. For instance, he sends you rain and good crops and gives you food and joyful hearts." But even with these words, Paul and Barnabas could scarcely restrain the people from sacrificing to them.

Acts 14:8-18 (NLT)

In Lystra, Paul and Barnabas were hailed as "gods in human form," by the crowd. In Ovid's *Metamorphoses*, one legend is that Zeus and Hermes actually came to this region as humans but were not recognized or welcomed. Perhaps this mob didn't want a repeat of that, so they repurposed the temple sacrifices toward Paul and Barnabas. The people brought gifts and flowers and were even going to sacrifice an offering to them. Paul and Barnabas did not take the accolades, and they didn't take the gesture lightly. They were dismayed and tore their clothing. Tearing one's clothing is an ancient Jewish tradition depicting humility, grief, loss, and disgust. These two leaders wanted nothing of these tributes. Paul and Barnabas shouted their objections. The leaders didn't accept the praise, they did all they could to stop it.

Peter had a similar encounter:

The next day Peter started out with them, and some of the believers from Joppa went along. The following day he arrived in Caesarea. Cornelius was expecting them and had called together his relatives and close friends. As Peter entered the house, Cornelius met him and fell at his feet in reverence. But Peter made him get up. "Stand up," he said, "I am only a man myself."

Acts 10:24-26 (NIV)

Often we don't stop folks from going over the top with their praise for our leadership or sermonizing. We accept it, and perhaps some of us crave it. Has our church culture over-hyped the praise of men so much that we think receiving it is the primary goal in preaching?

Jim Putman admitted, "The job of the Pastor was never to be the paid entertainer."

Barnabas and Paul acted in extreme contrast to another leader just two chapters prior:

Now Herod was very angry with the people of Tyre and Sidon. So they sent a delegation to make peace with him because their cities were dependent upon Herod's country for food. The delegates won the support of Blastus, Herod's personal assistant, and an appointment with Herod was granted. When the day arrived, Herod put on his royal robes, sat on his throne, and made a speech to them. The people gave him a great ovation, shouting, "It's the voice of a god, not of a man!"

Instantly, an angel of the Lord struck Herod with a sickness, because he accepted the people's worship instead of giving the glory to God. So he was consumed with worms and died.

Meanwhile, the word of God continued to spread, and there were many new believers.

Acts 12:20-24 (NLT)

Herod Agrippa accepted the worship instead of giving glory to God. The result: he was eaten by worms and died.

One of the hazards of preaching is people may go overboard on their praise. They may slip from worshiping the Creator into worshiping the creature, the servant, the preacher.

John Madden warned, "Self-praise is for losers. Be a winner. Stand for something. Always have class, and be humble."

We have got to be careful, intentional, and take every precaution not to accept accolades meant for someone else. We should not worm our way into receiving God's glory, or we may end up with worms.

Another story from the Book of Acts shows us why grabbing for praise is a losing proposition:

Once we were safe on shore, we learned that we were on the island of Malta. The people of the island were very kind to us. It was cold and rainy, so they built a fire on the shore to welcome us.

Acts 28:1-2 (NLT)

Paul had just survived a shipwreck by swimming to shore.

As Paul gathered an armful of sticks and was laying them on the fire, a poisonous snake, driven out

> by the heat, bit him on the hand. The people of
> the island saw it hanging from his hand and said
> to each other, "A murderer, no doubt! Though he
> escaped the sea, justice will not permit him to live."
>
> Acts 28:3-4 (NLT)

Talk about having a bad day – Paul goes from ship-wreck to snakebite. So the crowd immediately assumes that Paul must be a bad dude because fate won't let him go. They instantaneously label him a murderer.

> But Paul shook off the snake into the fire and was
> unharmed. The people waited for him to swell up
> or suddenly drop dead. But when they had waited
> a long time and saw that he wasn't harmed, they
> changed their minds and decided he was a god.
>
> Acts 13:5-6 (NLT)

Paul shook off the nasty snake, and apparently the nasty label, and when nothing traumatic happened, the crowd switched from calling him a murderer to calling him a god.

Here's the point: The crowd is full of crap!

The mob, more often than not, doesn't really know what they are talking about. Don't listen to the masses. They can turn from wanting you killed to wanting you crowned in a matter of a minute.

Amazingly, the Apostle Paul himself may have succumbed to caring too much about what the crowd thought. After his shipwreck and snake incident, the Book of Acts tells this story:

Three days after Paul's arrival, he called together the local Jewish leaders. He said to them, "Brothers, I was arrested in Jerusalem and handed over to the Roman government, even though I had done nothing against our people or the customs of our ancestors. The Romans tried me and wanted to release me, because they found no cause for the death sentence. But when the Jewish leaders protested the decision, I felt it necessary to appeal to Caesar, even though I had no desire to press charges against my own people. I asked you to come here today so we could get acquainted and so I could explain to you that I am bound with this chain because I believe that the hope of Israel – the Messiah – has already come."

Acts 28:17-20 (NLT)

Paul finally gets to Rome, and then he calls the local leaders together to give his explanation as to why he was in chains. But look at their response:

They replied, "We have had no letters from Judea or reports against you from anyone who has come here" (Acts 28:21, NLT).

The crowd is full of crap, but don't concern yourself with them – they probably aren't actually talking about you that much anyway!

Paul must have learned that lesson, because later he wrote:

And I, when I came to you, brothers, did not come proclaiming to you the testimony of God with lofty speech or wisdom. For I decided to know nothing among you except Jesus Christ and him crucified. And I was with you in weakness and in fear and much trembling, and my speech and my message were not in plausible words of wisdom, but in demonstration of the Spirit and of power, so that your faith might not rest in the wisdom of men but in the power of God.

1 Corinthians 2:1-5 (ESV)

Paul also wrote this instruction:

Let us not be ambitious for our own reputation for that only means making each other jealous.

Galatians 5:26 (Phillips)

Jesus had a similar warning for his disciples:

The seventy-two returned with joy and said, "Lord, even the demons submit to us in your name." He replied, "I saw Satan fall like lightning from heaven. I have given you authority to trample on snakes and scorpions and to overcome all the power of the enemy; nothing will harm you. However, do not rejoice that the spirits submit to you, but rejoice that your names are written in heaven."

Luke 10:17-20 (NIV)

Earthly accolades don't mean much, a heavenly home does.

When English Playwright Oscar Wilde arrived at his club late at night after witnessing the first presentation of a play that had been a complete failure, someone asked. "How did your play go tonight, Oscar?" "Oh," said Wilde, "the play was a great success. The audience was a failure."

It doesn't matter all that much what the crowd says, so let's shun the accolades, and leave the glory for God.

The Best Comment

It happens just about every Sunday, just about every time I preach or speak at an event or function. When I finish presenting, I sneak to the back of the room, right by the exit, and I shake hands with people as they leave. Most people know the drill. They are supposed to say, "Nice sermon, Pastor." That's the secret code. That is the church

It's easy to get caught up in the notion that it is about us.

world's equivalent to, "The crow flies at midnight!" – it is the closest thing to a password to get you out the door. Over the years I've heard lots of comments from folks on their way out. I've heard a ton of "Nice sermon, Pastor" comments. Most remarks have been encouraging, some contain backhanded corrections, and every once in a while, people get downright nasty.

But there is one comment I've heard that is by far the best remark ever to come my way. There is one top comment, and no other comment even comes in as a close second. I've heard this comment three times in my three-plus decades of speaking – once over ten years ago, once about five years ago, and once this past year. There is one comment that has been the best comment I ever heard after speaking.

Here it is: "Are you Tricia's dad? Tricia is awesome!"

That's the best comment I've ever heard after speaking. Why was that comment so meaningful to me?

1. Because it's not about me. All three times I heard the comment about Tricia, I was startled and brought back to reality. It is not about me. A few years ago, noted author Max Lucado wrote a book titled *It's Not About Me.* I didn't read it, because, well, it's not about me!

It's easy to get caught up in the notion that it is about us. As preachers, presenters, we're artists, and each talk is a part of us. We're putting ourselves out there and we take each comment pretty personally. But when I was asked about Tricia, I was reminded to take myself less seriously.

I have received similar comments about my sons when they have preached at church, presented at a seminar, or led worship. I'd stand at the back and hear a lot of "You must be so proud" observations. But I expected those. Each time I was asked if I was Tricia's dad, Tricia wasn't even in the room. I was unexpectedly rebooted back to real life.

2. Because it's not about somebody else either. Tricia really is awesome. She's awesome in large part because she has an awesome mother. Tricia is awesome because as iron sharpens iron, she has allowed her brothers to sharpen her. Tricia is awesome because she has some great friends and teammates who have helped to "awesome her up." Tricia is awesome because she has had many mentors and coaches and teachers and church families that have helped shape her life.

But the "Tricia is awesome" line wasn't about them.

3. Because it's not even about Tricia. The first man who made this "Tricia comment" to me talked about how Tricia had been a big influence with his daughter. The second comment came from a college-aged girl who talked about how Tricia had spent many late nights talking and counseling with her, and how her life was now changed. The third remark came after I spoke to Tricia's missionary teammates in a far eastern country. I remember them talking initially about Tricia, but they went on to talk more about how God was working and the Kingdom was spreading and something powerful was at work.

4. Because it's about God. When I heard, "Are you Tricia's dad? Tricia is awesome!" I sensed the awesomeness of God. He is alive and working in ways we may never know, in people we may never meet and in places we may never see. It was amazingly encouraging to me to get a glimpse of multiplication, to get a sense of reproduction, and to experience the Kingdom of God expanding.

> For the LORD Most High is awesome...
> Psalm 47:2 (NIV)

God really is awesome! Let's leave all the glory for him.

MINI CASE STUDY:
HIGH DESERT CHURCH, VICTORVILLE, CALIFORNIA

Pastor Tom Mercer says, "A Teaching Team is part of 'exponential thinking.' I've often said that just because you have multiple staff members doesn't mean you have a staff team. Right now, we're in a season of succession (new senior leadership). Sharing weekend responsibilities, as a matter of long-term strategy, is a key component to the 'old guy' not being missed when he's gone. I could now leave for a couple of months at a time and doubt that very many people would miss me."

High Desert generates the live presentation from their original campus, which is streamed to the other campuses seventy percent of the time. The Campus Lead Pastors teach live at their sites monthly.

The Team is comprised of the Pastor to Campuses, Senior Pastor, Campus Leads, each campus worship staff, Small Groups Pastor, and Com Team designer (whichever one's been assigned to the series). Regardless of who is teaching, they are all expected to attend the meeting each week.

"More seasoned champions of orthodox theology" are also invited to read submitted scripts and participate in the meetings as they are able.

At the teaching team meeting, the members discuss the prior weekend's presentation (positives and negatives), the upcoming weekend's initial script, and then brainstorm ideas for the message looming on the following weekend.

High Desert presently has three primary preachers, plus the Lead Pastors, who speak eleven or twelve times per year. The Senior Pastor speaks approximately twenty-four to twenty-eight times per year, the two other members speak six to eight times each. "Expert" guests do two to four messages and the campus leads teach live at their site eleven to twelve times.

Mercer lists these advantages and downsides of team teaching:

Advantages:

- We believe variety (to a point) is beneficial.
- We value ethnic balance in our weekend presentations.
- We believe the Holy Spirit has gifted most (if not all) churches with multiple teachers.
- If the Senior Pastor was removed by tragedy or illness, the church is prepared to respond.
- No more last-minute message prep!

Disadvantages:

- Pastors have to get over themselves. That's an upside, but it can feel like a downside.
- It takes a lot of work and preparation to mobilize a group to do anything.

THE BIG CHALLENGE:

Take time to determine when and by whom you are most likely to fall prey to the "celebrity syndrome." What is one strategy to help you maintain humility and be intentional about not letting the praise of the fickle crowds go to your head?

PART TWO

WHAT?

CHAPTER 5

ON A MISSION

No member of a crew is praised for the rugged individuality of his rowing.

—Ralph Waldo Emerson

The best way to find out if you can trust somebody is to trust them.

—Ernest Hemingway

God does not give churches to leaders, he gives leaders to churches.

—Leonce Crump

At one point during a game, the coach said to one of his young players, "Do you understand what cooperation is? What a team is?" The little boy nodded yes. "Do you understand that what matters is whether we win together as a team?" The little boy nodded yes. "So," the coach continued, "when a penalty is called, or you disagree, you don't argue or curse or attack the referee. Do you understand all that?" Again, the boy nodded yes. "Good," said the coach. "Now go over there and explain it to your mother."

What constitutes a team? If we're going to develop a teaching team, what would it look like?

A couple years ago my daughter, Tricia, delivered a presentation on what makes an effective team based on her missions work in a foreign country – which we're not supposed to talk about, so I won't mention the name.

Tricia mentioned three elements of teams on a mission:

1. Clearly defined roles.

Tricia teaches at a University in a remote city. She works on a team with other missionaries, and they have learned if they want to be effective they must team up with the local underground church.

On day one in their new city, Tricia visited the pastor of a local church located just outside the college campus where she teaches.

As they talked through philosophies, priorities, and roles, Tricia and the pastor came to an understanding. The foreign missions team would be focusing primarily on evangelism – leading students to Jesus. That is the expertise of the missionaries. The underground church would focus primarily on spiritual growth – helping the new believers grow closer to Jesus. That is the passion of the pastor.

Without a high degree of mutual dependence and reliance, teams break down.

The clarification of roles reduced insecurity and competition, and immediately fostered cooperation.

2. High levels of trust

Tricia admitted to being amazed that during her very first meeting with this local church pastor, he handed her a set of keys to the church facility. This underground church is located on the sixth floor of an apartment building!

Teams disintegrate without trust. Without a high degree of mutual dependence and reliance, teams break down.

3. Dangerous tasks

Tricia admitted, "One questionable word to the authorities from him and I will be kicked out of the country. One questionable word to the authorities from me and he will go to jail."

Her conclusion: "Do you want to unite your team? Do something illegal together!"

Strong teams don't form so much from eating ice cream together as they do from jointly discharging dangerous, challenging, world-changing missions.

What does a teaching team look like? An effective team would embody all three of the characteristics Tricia mentioned:

An effective teaching team includes clearly defined roles.

It appears in the Book of Acts that roles were defined and understood.

> Barnabas they called Zeus, and Paul they called Hermes because he was the chief speaker.
>
> Acts 14:12(NIV)

Paul and Barnabas started with defined roles – Paul was the chief speaker. Perhaps their breakup in Acts 15 stemmed from a lack of role definition regarding who was in charge of partner recruiting.

But they seemed to understand that Paul was the lead speaker.

The Pitching Staff

I'm not sure if I heard the analogy first from Larry Osborne or Jeff Sammons. Both described teaching teams as a sort of pitching rotation.

(Osborne says if you go to Dodger Stadium, you don't have to go when their best pitcher is starting to enjoy the experience. You can have a great time regardless of who is pitching. He contrasts that to attending a Broadway Play. If you learn that the star of the show is not performing, you are disappointed that you have to sit through it watching the understudy. I like the National Football League comparison. Most churches see their Senior Pastor as the starting quarterback. If the starter isn't playing, there is a huge difference in quality to the "back-up," so it may not be worth the price of a ticket.)

We often define the roles on our church's teaching team along the lines of a baseball team's pitching staff.

On just about any baseball team you will find *the ace of the staff*, also known as the lead dog, or the number one starter. This person takes the ball on opening day, for big games, and if schedules allow, the first game of any playoff series.

The Lead Pastor would typically still be the number one starter on any teaching team. The ace would probably plan on speaking on Easter, Christmas Eve, and most big days.

Next is *the number two starter*. Some fortunate teams have two strong pitchers they refer to as 1 and 1A. We try to train our speakers so there isn't a huge drop-off from the Lead Pastor to the next person. Our number two and number three starters don't miss a beat.

A common responsibility for *the third and fourth starters* on a typical pitching staff is to "eat up innings." These players are not always expected to be as capable as the lead pitcher, but they allow the ace to get some rest and not have to carry the entire burden.

Most Major League Baseball pitching staffs have *a fifth starter*. This pitcher is not expected to pitch as much as the primary players, but this is a meaningful role. We see the fifth starter as someone who can handle lower attendance days.

Then there is the *long reliever*. This pitcher comes into play when a starter falters early, or a health or crisis issue causes the starter to not be able to go. Do you have someone ready to come in if the scheduled speaker cannot make it due to illness, emergency, or crisis?

Most teams also have *middle-inning relievers*. These pitchers typically come in for the fifth, sixth, or seventh innings of a nine-inning contest. Their role is to keep the lead or keep the game close. We have some folks who excel at giving one point in the middle of the message. Their role isn't to carry the entire sermon, but to keep the flow of the message going by delivering one or two points of the talk.

The *left-handed relief specialist* is often called upon to face just one or two batters. On a teaching team, perhaps there is someone whose primary role is to give one, quick word of wisdom. Or perhaps there is someone on your team who can speak as an expert on one topic on several different occasions (such as financial management or prayer).

Another role is the *Rule Five Player*. Major League Baseball institutes an amateur draft where high school, college, and some international players are selected by professional teams. MLB also has another draft:

"Rule 5 Draft: A MLB player draft that occurs each year during the Winter Meetings of General Managers. The Rule 5 draft aims to prevent teams from stockpiling too many young players on their minor league affiliate teams when other teams would be willing to have them play in the majors...Players chosen in the Rule 5 draft must remain on that team's 25-man roster for one full season or be offered back to the previous team..."[16]

Perhaps there is a potential teacher in your midst who isn't ready to be up front speaking, but having this person on your team allows them to develop as they hang around your current teachers. If you don't bring them on your team, you might actually lose them.

Most baseball teams have their best relief pitcher serve as *the closer*. This pitcher comes into the end of the game, usually the ninth inning, to close out the game and preserve a win for the team.

In our church, the Lead Pastor, Tim Pearring, serves as the closer on those occasions when he isn't preaching. Tim takes the stage immediately after the message. After he encourages the speaker, Tim highlights the sermon and ties it into the vision and values of the church.

I've been asked if having a larger teaching team diminishes the spiritual authority of the pastor. With Tim closing

---

16 "MLB Draft Rules," DraftSite: The Original Full Round Mock Draft Site, accessed November 22, 2018, https://www.draftsite.com/mlb/rules/.

out each message, I believe this approach actually enhances his leadership when he isn't preaching. (If you are familiar with Andy Stanley's, "Me-We-God-You-We" format, Tim does the "We" portion of the message as the closer.)

Another often overlooked position on the pitching staff is the *bullpen catcher*. This unheralded role player never gets into the game or even on the active roster, but performs the task of warming up relief pitchers during the game and maybe also starting pitchers before the game.

Casey Chavez has been a bullpen catcher for the Oakland A's for nine-plus seasons. He's never played an actual game at that level. Recently he was asked by a reporter, "Don't you ever wish you could experience that MLB-level intensity inside the foul lines?"

Chavez responded, "When I went to college, I'd already stopped playing, and then I discovered the coaching side of it. I just had more energy on that side of the game than I ever did as a player. I can't really tell you why other than I feel like maybe this is something I was born to do. But I enjoyed playing just as much as anybody else; I had dreamed of playing as much as anybody else. The work that I wasn't willing to put in as a player, for whatever reason, I was willing to put in on the coaching side. So being on that side of the game and not holding on to that player hope or the player dream, I had a different work ethic. And when they asked me to learn how to catch, I was fixated on doing it and I worked as hard as I could; I talked to as

> **There may be people in your ministry who will never preach on stage, but they can be incredibly valuable.**

many people as I could; I studied the position as much as I could, and I'm still doing it!"

There may be people in your ministry who will never preach on stage, but they can be incredibly valuable from the coaching side of the team.

That leads to the last role: *the pitching coach*. This person trains and mentors the team's pitchers. He advises the manager on the condition of pitchers and their arms and serves as an in-game adviser for the pitcher currently on the mound.

I serve as the primary coach for the teachers on our team. I try to instruct and mentor them and advise the manager – I mean Lead Pastor – on how the teachers are progressing.

In addition to these roles on a Major League roster, professional baseball teams also have farm systems, where *farm team pitchers* – potential players – are developed and coached toward growth in their profession. We have two types of teaching team meetings in our church – one that meets to work through schedules and messages, and another team that works with newer, budding presenters.

Certainly, you may not expect to have all these roles filled on your ministry team. You might just have one or two other people involved. But a team has to have more than one person on it. It's been said, "There is no 'I' in team!" It's also been said, "I know, but there's an 'M' and an 'E,' so I don't need anyone else." Yes, you do.

Putting together a teaching team means discovering appropriate roles for your ministry and slotting folks into those positions.

An effective teaching team includes high levels of trust.

Teamwork is essential – it allows you to blame some-one else.

But effective teamwork requires trust.

One day a wife said to her husband, "You won't believe this, but our weekend guests stole four of our best towels." "Well," answered the husband, "some people are like that. You can't trust them, they're just made that way. By the way, which ones did they get?" The wife said, "They stole those fluffy white ones with Hyatt Regency written on them!"

It is difficult to trust people, especially after we've been burned a few times. An old quote goes, "People ask me why it's so hard to trust people, I ask them, 'Why is it so hard to keep a promise?'"

Trust is difficult. But the Book of Acts is filled with leaders who trusted other people.

Barnabas trusted Paul when no one else would:

> When Saul arrived in Jerusalem, he tried to meet with the believers, but they were all afraid of him. They did not believe he had truly become a believer! Then Barnabas brought him to the apostles and told them how Saul had seen the Lord on the way to Damascus and how the Lord had spoken to Saul. He also told them that Saul had preached boldly in the name of Jesus in Damascus.
>
> Acts 9:26-27 (NLT)

It's amazing to me that immediately after Paul and Barnabas had their sharp disagreement, Paul found Timothy.

Paul went first to Derbe and then to Lystra, where there was a young disciple named Timothy. His mother was a Jewish believer, but his father was a Greek. Timothy was well thought of by the believers in Lystra and Iconium, so Paul wanted him to join them on their journey. In deference to the Jews of the area, he arranged for Timothy to be circumcised before they left, for everyone knew that his father was a Greek.

Acts 16:1-3 (NLT)

What is even more amazing is that Timothy allowed Paul to circumcise him.

The clear environment of trust is one of the primary causes of church expansion through the early disciples.

Master collaborator Nathan "Chivo" Hawkins says, "Trust is the foundation collaboration is built upon."

Amber Harding concluded, "Contrary to popular belief, there most certainly is an "I" in "team." It is the same "I" that appears three times in "responsibility."[17]

Booker T. Washington put it this way, "Few things help an individual more than to place responsibility upon him, and to let him know that you trust him."

Peter Drucker observed, "The leaders who work most effectively, it seems to me, never say 'I.' And that's not because they have trained themselves not to say 'I.' They don't think 'I.' They think 'we;' they think 'team.' They understand their job to be to make the team function. They

---

17 "Allison Clark's Blog," accessed November 22, 2018, https://alleyclark.wordpress.com/.

accept responsibility and don't sidestep it, but 'we' gets the credit.... This is what creates trust, what enables you to get the task done."[18]

Developing a teaching team means we must learn to trust other people. The authors of *Extreme Ownership* conclude their book with this:

> A leader has nothing to prove, but everything to prove. By virtue of rank and position, the team understands that the leader is in charge. A good leader does not gloat or revel in his or her position. To take charge of minute details just to demonstrate and reinforce to the team a leader's authority is the mark of poor, inexperienced leadership lacking in confidence. Since the team understands that the leader is de facto in charge, in that respect, a leader has nothing to prove. But in another respect, a leader has everything to prove: every member of the team must develop the trust and confidence that their leader will exercise good judgment, remain calm, and make the right decisions when it matters most. Leaders must earn that respect and prove themselves worthy, demonstrating through action that they will take care of the team and look out for their long-term interests and well-being. In that respect, a leader has everything to prove every day.[19]

---

18 "Peter F. Drucker," Citaty.net, accessed November 22, 2018, https://citaty.net/citaty/889889-peter-f-drucker-the-leaders-who-work-most-effectively.

19 Willink and Babin, *Extreme Ownership*, 277.

An effective teaching team involves dangerous tasks

> As soon as there is life there is danger.
> —Ralph Waldo Emerson

One day at the veterinarian's office a man and the receptionist were verbally sparring. Things became quite heated, and after a few tense moments, a technician came to the receptionist's defense. "Sir," she interjected, "are you aware of what happens to aggressive males in this office?"

Life is dangerous.

Helen Keller observed, "Security is mostly a superstition. It does not exist in nature, nor do the children of men as a whole experience it. Avoiding danger is no safer in the long run than outright exposure. Life is either a daring adventure, or nothing."

> When I'm driving here I see a sign that says,
> CAUTION: SMALL CHILDREN PLAYING. I
> slow down, and then it occurs to me, I'm not afraid
> of small children.
> —Jonathan Katz

Maybe you're not afraid of preaching. Perhaps you should be.

Preaching is dangerous. My Dad was a civil engineer. He used to joke, "A doctor buries his mistakes. A lawyer's mistakes end up in prison. But a civil engineer's mistakes are there in the open for everyone to see." When I became a pastor, I joked back, "Dad, a preacher's mistakes end up in hell."

Preaching can be dangerous. Just look at Paul's trials:

> I have worked harder, been put in prison more often, been whipped times without number, and faced death again and again. Five different times the Jewish leaders gave me thirty-nine lashes. Three times I was beaten with rods. Once I was stoned. Three times I was shipwrecked. Once I spent a whole night and a day adrift at sea. I have traveled on many long journeys. I have faced danger from rivers and from robbers. I have faced danger from my own people, the Jews, as well as from the Gentiles. I have faced danger in the cities, in the deserts, and on the seas. And I have faced danger from men who claim to be believers but are not. I have worked hard and long, enduring many sleepless nights. I have been hungry and thirsty and have often gone without food. I have shivered in the cold, without enough clothing to keep me warm.
>
> 2 Corinthians 11:24-27 (NLT)

The message is clear: Do not get on a boat with the Apostle Paul! And realize that when you invite other people into the preaching ministry, you are inviting them into a dangerous mission.

In his book, *Tortured for Christ*, Richard Wurmbrand recalls, "It was strictly forbidden to preach to other prisoners. It was understood that whoever was caught doing this received a severe beating. A number of us decided to pay the price for the privilege of preaching, so we accepted their (the communists) terms. It was a deal; we preached and they beat us. We were happy preaching. They were happy beating us, so everyone was happy." [20]

"Newspapers called it the 'Dance of Danger' – bridge construction on top of swaying catwalks and high towers, sometimes hundreds of feet in the air, blown by ill winds. This dance had even yielded a calculated fatality rate: For every one million dollars spent, one life would be lost. That was what officials could expect.

Danger can unite us as a team like nothing else, and surviving danger together can help us become even more productive.

Engineers on the Golden Gate Bridge, however, believed the risks could be lowered. When construction began in 1932, numerous safety measures were put into place and strictly enforced: mandatory use of hard hats, prescription-filtered eye glasses, no show-boating (cause for automatic firing), tie-off lines, and an on-site hospital helped to greatly reduce the casualty rate. After nearly four years of construction and $20 million spent, only one worker had died. The most effective safety device, without question, was as new to bridge building as it was old to the circus: the use of a trapeze net. This large net cost $130,000 and draped sixty feet below the roadbed under construction, extending ten feet to either side. So effective

---

20   Richard Wurmbrand, George Verwer, and Dale Rhoton, *Tortured for Christ* (Colorado Springs, CO: David C Cook, 2017).

was the safety net that the newspapers began running box scores: 'Score on the Gate Bridge Safety Net to Date: 8 Lives Saved!' Those men whose lives had been delivered by the net were said to have joined the 'Halfway to Hell Club.' Beyond that, the net had another significant benefit: it freed many of the workers from an often-paralyzing sense of fear. And that, many said, helped them work more productively."[21]

Danger can unite us as a team like nothing else, and surviving danger together can help us become even more productive.

What does a teaching team look like? It looks like an environment of mission.

MINI-CASE STUDY:
REFUGE, LONG BEACH, CALIFORNIA

Self-described Church Planting Ninja Peyton Jones started the church with an Ephesians 4 mindset. He served as an apostle, but looked for a prophet, evangelist, pastor and teacher for his teaching team. All five different leader types mentioned in that foundational Bible chapter serve to help the believers. Currently there is a team of seven to eight speakers.

Preachers are rotated. The apostle did most of the preaching at the beginning because of missional and kingdom advancement priorities. Now the teacher does the

---

21   Robert Lewis and Rob Wilkins, *The Church of Irresistible Influence* (Grand Rapids, MI: Zondervan Pub. House, 2001), 140-141.

lion's share. The teacher speaks twice a month with the others filling in the gaps, sometimes newbies rotate in to speak five to ten minutes of a message.

Potential speakers come out of the discipleship process and primarily through small groups. Leaders are trained to look for teaching gifts during conversations. Jones writes, "You create a leadership pipeline. The believers hear from different teaching styles and giftings (prophetic, shepherd, teacher, etc.). You have ready-made team leaders ready to go!"

Jones implements training retreats for preachers/teachers.

Lesson Details: Seven classes cover essential elements of the preacher's character, preparation, and delivery. They focus on seven core lessons:

The Heart of Teaching - Ezra 7 & Nehemiah 8
The Calling of the Teacher - 2 Corinthians 2:17, 3:5-6
The Heart of the Teacher - 2 Corinthians 5
The Integrity of the Teacher - Daniel 6
The Holy Spirit in the Teacher - Acts 1:4-8, 2 Corinthians 3-4
Sacred Trust - 2 Timothy 1:13-14
Welcome to the Fight - 1 Timothy 6:12, Colossians 1:28-2:1

Each class is followed by hands-on preparation of essential Bible-teaching elements.

Students will receive immediate feedback, and learn from one another as they listen, critique, and encourage each other. Jones concludes, "So leave your ego at home and show up ready to learn!"

Peyton cites the downsides of team teaching as a lack of consistency, and, "If people are carnal, they "follow Apollos," or "Cephas."

THE BIG CHALLENGE:

Identify which positions on your pitching staff are presently filled, and which positions are currently empty. Set a goal to fill at least one of the empty positions within a specific period of time.

CHAPTER 6

A WING AND A PRAYER

Teaching can be the easiest job in the world. But if you do it right, it is the hardest job in the world.

—Jeff Sammons

A prepared messenger is more important than a prepared message.

—Robert Munger

Some ministers are capable of giving the impression that they were informed only five minutes ago that it was Sunday.

—Fred Craddock

"This is going to be the most difficult college course you will ever take," the speech instructor warned our standing-room-only class on day one. "You will wish you were taking that weed-out-the-pre-med-students anatomy class everyone complains about. I will pile up your homework assignments so high, you will dread you ever signed up and stayed in this speech class." The professor sternly recounted her days writing speeches for "a very famous California governor who used to be an actor," and how difficult writing, preparing, and delivering speeches is – especially under her tutelage. Her aim appeared to be to scare most of us out of taking her class. It turned out, that was exactly what she was attempting. Only twelve of us showed up the next class meeting.

She started day two by apologizing for her harsh words on the first day, explaining that too many students had enrolled and she needed to pare down the num- bers. She took the exact same approach for her advanced speech course that I took the following semester. In actuality, this teacher was a sweetheart, she loved her students and her classes were my favorite ones at UCLA. But her first-day warnings did contain a ton of truth – speaking is hard work.

What does a teaching team look like? It looks like hard work.

> Each Sabbath found Paul at the synagogue, trying to convince the Jews and Greeks alike. And after Silas and Timothy came down from Macedonia, Paul spent all his time preaching the word. He testified to the Jews that Jesus was the Messiah.
>
> Acts 18:4-5 (NLT)

Paul spent, "all his time" working on his messages. The Phillips version says he was immersed in his work:

> By the time Silas and Timothy arrived from Macedonia Paul was completely absorbed in preaching the message, showing the Jews as clearly as he could that Jesus is Christ.
>
> Acts 18:4-5 (Phillips)

Again, we see the clear markings of diligence in Paul's messages:

> Then Paul made his way into the synagogue there and for three months he spoke with the utmost confidence, using both argument and persuasion as he talked of the kingdom of God.
>
> Acts 19:8 (Phillips)

At the end of the Book of Acts we see Paul continuing to work carefully at preaching:

> He explained and testified about the Kingdom of God and tried to persuade them about Jesus from the Scriptures. Using the law of Moses and the books of the prophets, he spoke to them from morning until evening.
>
> Acts 28:23 (NLT)

Later Paul wrote this to Timothy:

> "Until I come, devote yourself to the public reading of Scripture, to preaching and to teaching."
>
> 1 Timothy 4:13 (NIV)

What does a teaching team look like? It looks like hard work. Developing a teaching team means moving beyond the comfort zone to be much more intentional about the task.

John Stott, in his book *The Challenge of Preaching* admits, "A low level of Christian living is due, more than anything else, to a low level of Christian preaching. If the church is to flourish again, there is a need for faithful, powerful, biblical preaching. God still urges his people to listen and his preachers to proclaim his word."[22]

Tim Notke says, "Hard work beats talent, when talent doesn't work hard."

Wayne McDill wrote in *The 12 Essential Skills for Great Preaching*, "Preaching is not an easy assignment. In every generation someone declares that preaching as we have always known it is a thing of the past. Alternatives are suggested that will be much more effective – counseling, drama, audiovisual media, lectures using PowerPoint. Words from the ancient book of Ecclesiastes are still true today for the work of the faithful preacher: 'And moreover, because the Preacher was wise, he still taught the people knowledge; yes, he pondered and sought out and set in order many proverbs. The Preacher sought to find acceptable words; and what was written was upright – words of truth' (Ecclesiastes 12:9-10, NKJV)." [23]

Preaching requires diligence. Preaching as a team requires team diligence.

That great preacher Solomon added:

> Lazy people want much but get little, but those who work hard will prosper.
>
> Proverbs 13:4 (NLT)

---

22   John R. W. Stott and Greg Scharf, *The Challenge of Preaching* (Grand Rapids, MI: William B. Eerdmans Publishing Company, 2015).

23   Wayne McDill, *12 Essential Skills for Great Preaching*, 2nd ed. (Nashville, TN: B & H Publishing Group, 2018), Kindle Edition, Locations 129-134.

Good planning and hard work lead to prosperity,
but hasty shortcuts lead to poverty.

> Proverbs 21:5 (NLT)

Mark Twain quipped, "It takes three weeks to prepare an impromptu speech."

Preaching requires diligence. Preaching as a team requires team diligence. And preaching as a team helps ensure diligence. A teaching team helps with intentionality and industriousness in speaking.

The team pushes us back to the passage.

One phrase you will consistently hear in our teaching team meetings is, "The power comes from the passage."

Haddon Robinson put it this way, "Yet when they fail to preach the Scriptures, they abandon their authority."

Tim Challies discovered, "According to a new study by Gallup, the hottest thing at church today is not the worship and not the pastor. It's not the smoke and lights and it's not the hip and relevant youth programs. It's not even the organic, fair trade coffee at the cafe. The hottest thing at church today is the preaching. Not only is it the preaching, but a very specific form of it – preaching based on the Bible."

I recently attended a national gathering for leaders. Big time preachers were called in for the keynote messages. One of the speakers was tasked with the challenge of preaching on empowerment. I had not heard of this person, and I was startled to hear him speak about how King Saul empowered David by giving the boy his kingly armor. The speaker was entertaining. He started to shake, he threw out rhymes, he arranged for a keyboard player to come on stage and accompany his preaching with background organ music. The crowd went wild, almost everyone stood and applauded.

I sat dumbfounded. King Saul empowered David? I wondered if anyone else in the auditorium had actually ever read that story. Saul didn't empower, he abdicated his leadership. 1 Samuel 17:37 reads, *"Saul finally consented..."* This was like saying Richard Nixon empowered Gerald Ford.

The speaker could have used a number of biblical stories to get the point across because it is actually a biblical principle – we're called to empower others. But he chose to make himself look good instead of allowing the power to come from the passage. He didn't do his work.

Fred Craddock was once asked the key to preaching. He replied, "First, read the passage." Then he added, "Too many preachers prepare an entire sermon without looking at the biblical text."

Recently our church was working through a series on Luke chapter 4. One of the speakers walked through his talk with us. It was well thought out, well crafted and well done, but every other person on the team raised the same question, "Where is Luke chapter 4 in your message? Nice talk, but where is the passage?" The speaker agreed, apologized, and made the appropriate changes. The power comes from the passage.

When we utilize a team for collaboration or simply running the message by them in advance, the team can bring us back to the passage. The temptation is to use the passage as a spring board to get to our opinions, or even jump to other passages. A team working together helps keep us biblical and orthodox.

The team encourages us to put in the time

We can slide by on our talent alone for a while, but unless we work at developing it, we're not going to get very far.

Calvin Miller wrote, "Becoming a great preacher, like becoming a great artist, requires a life commitment."

D. A. Carson added, "There is no long range, effective teaching of the Bible that is not accompanied by long hours of ongoing study of the Bible."

Teaching takes time

Comedian Steven Wright observed, "I watched the Indy 500, and I was thinking that if they left earlier they wouldn't have to go so fast."

Shortcuts don't play well in the pulpit.

Seth Godin wrote about "The Myth of Quick":

> In his day job, The Wizard of Oz sold hokum. Patent medicines guaranteed to cure what ailed you. And none of them worked.
>
> Deep within each of us is the yearning for the pill, the neck crack, the organizational re-do that will fix everything.
>
> Sometimes, it even happens. Sometimes, once in a very rare while, there actually is a stone in our shoe, easy to remove. And this rare occurrence serves to encourage our dreams that all of our

problems have such a simple diagnosis and an even simpler remedy.

Alas, it's not true.

Culture takes years to create and years to change.

Illnesses rarely respond in days to a treatment.

Organizations that are drowning need to learn to swim.

Habits beat interventions every time.

Consider these boundaries...

Avoid the crash diet.

Fear the stock that's a sure thing to double overnight.

Be skeptical of a new technology that's surely revolutionary.

Walk away from a consultant who can transform your organization in one fell swoop.

Your project (and your health) is too valuable to depend on lottery tickets.

There are innovations and moments that lead to change. But that change happens over time, with new rules causing new outputs that compound. The instant win is largely a myth.

The essential elements of a miracle are that it is rare and unpredictable. Not quite the reliable path you were seeking.[24]

When we move to team teaching, we are forced to become even more intentional about putting in the time

---

24   https://seths.blog/2016/12/the-myth-of-quick/

and the work and the effort because we know they can tell if we're just winging it.

Do you think Barnabas was going to slothfully deliver a "Saturday Night Special" with Paul on his team? I don't think so.

The team helps us share the work.

I suspect that many preachers finish their last preaching class and never really get help the rest of their preaching lives. No wonder so many of us struggle.

University of Kentucky basketball coach John Calipari made an amazing admission about what he tells his players: "'You've got to love the grind.' That's something they probably hear from me more than anything else. You've got to love the grind. Embrace the work. Embrace the sweat. Embrace the pain."[25]

Christmas was finally over and the Pastor's wife dropped into an easy chair saying, "Boy! Am I ever tired." Her husband looked over at her and said, "I had to conduct two special services last night, three today, and give a total of five sermons. Why are you so tired?"

"Dear," she replied, "I had to listen to all of them."

The team not only encourages us toward hard work, they help carry the load.

Charles Swindoll wrote, "Preachers have a saying: 'Sunday comes every three days!' Whenever I quote it, fellow preachers invariably respond with a knowing laugh…

---

25 John Calipari, *Players First: Coaching from the inside out* (NY, NY: Penguin Press, 2015), Kindle Edition, 101.

Like a lumbering freight train, Sunday morning rolls toward him with steady, relentless inevitability.[26]

A.B. Simpson said, "God has hidden every precious thing in such a way that it is a reward to the diligent, a prize to the earnest, but a disappointment to the slothful soul. All nature is arrayed against the lounger and the idler. The nut is hidden in its thorny case, the pearl is buried beneath the ocean waves; the gold is imprisoned in the rocky mountain; the gem is found only after you crush the rock which encloses it; the very soil gives its harvest as a reward to the laboring farmer."

Dr. Benjamin Bloom wrote a book called, *Teaching and Learning Conditions for Extreme Levels of Talent Development* (Obviously, picking titles isn't one of his strengths). He studied how long it takes to achieve world-class competency in a field. The study analyzed world-class concert pianists, sculptors, mathematicians, brain surgeons, Olympic athletes and tennis champions. Guess how long on average it took to become world class? The answer is between ten to seventeen years. For example, in a study of the winners of major international piano competitions, it was found that pianists worked 17.14 years from the day they began taking piano lessons to the day they won a major competition.

In his book *Outliers*, Malcom Gladwell discusses the research that concludes it takes an average of ten thousand hours of work for someone to become an expert in a topic or task.

---

26 Charles R. Swindoll, *Saying It Well: Touching Others with Your Words* (New York: FaithWords, 2012), Kindle Edition, 101.

The good news is with a good team we can count the hours and days – and even years – they help us as we seek to become proficient.

The team helps us make improvements.

John Wooden said, "The main ingredient in stardom is the rest of the team."

Teaching Cohort leader, Jim Kennon confessed, "After thirty-five years of preaching, I still find great benefit in gathering with a group of preachers who want to improve their skills. When one becomes proficient in their craft, it is easy to begin to accept the status quo. 'I've made it as a preacher and there is no need to improve.' Nothing could be further from the truth. Our cohort encourages me to sharpen my skills. It has pushed me to dedicate more time to honing my messages. Without a doubt, it has helped me raise my game."

> **Developing a teaching team breaks us out of our ruts, our mediocre patterns, our distracting mannerisms. We can become better if we work with others.**

Developing a teaching team breaks us out of our ruts, our mediocre patterns, our distracting mannerisms. We can become better if we work with others.

"None of us is as smart as all of us."

—Ken Blanchard

Carmine Gallo, in *The Presentation Secrets of Steve Jobs*, speaks to this:

"Steve Jobs spends hours rehearsing every facet of his presentation. Every slide is written like a piece of poetry, every presentation staged like a theatrical experience. Yes, Steve Jobs makes a presentation look effortless, but that polish comes after hours and hours of grueling practice. Steve Jobs has improved his style over time. If you watch video clips of Steve Jobs' presentations going back twenty years you will see that he improves significantly with every decade. The Steve Jobs of 1984 had a lot of charisma, but the Steve Jobs of 1997 was a far more polished speaker. The Steve Jobs who introduced the iPhone in 2007 was even better. Nobody is born knowing how to deliver a great PowerPoint presentation. Expert speakers hone that skill with practice."[27]

Charles Capps states, "I don't practice what I preach, I preach what I practice."

Practice is better in teams.

The team helps us know what to eliminate

My granddaughter, Hannah, just returned from a summer camp where she participated in a youth worship service. "How was the speaker," I asked. Hannah simply replied, "He talked for an hour and a half."

Some preachers use Acts 2:40 as their life verse: "Then Peter continued preaching for a long time…" (Acts 2:40, NLT).

---

27   "Peter F. Drucker," Citaty.net, accessed November 22, 2018, https://citaty.net/citaty/889889-peter-f-drucker-the-leaders-who-work-most-effectively.

The longest sermon on record was preached by Rev. Robert Marshall of Michigan in 1976. He preached for sixty hours and thirty-one minutes. The previous record holder was Robert McKee who spoke for fifty-two hours.

The great Charles Spurgeon offered this advice: "If you ask me how you may shorten your sermons, I should say, study them better... we are generally longest when we have least to say."

Michelangelo was asked about the difficulties he must have encountered on his greatest sculpture. He said, "It is easy. You just chip away the stone that doesn't look like David."

The only problem with that statement is chipping away isn't easy.

Mark Twain allegedly said, "I apologize for the length of this letter, but I didn't have time to make it shorter."

Carmine Gallo devotes an entire chapter in *Talk Like TED: The 9 Public-Speaking Secrets of the World's Top Minds* to presentation length. He concludes that eighteen minutes is the perfect amount of time for a talk:

> Dr. Paul King at Texas Christian University has been an influential scholar in the field of communication studies for thirty years. I spoke to King about his research into "state anxiety in listening performance." Most of us believe that anxiety impacts only the person giving the speech or presentation. Dr. King has discovered that audience members feel anxiety, too... King says that cognitive processing – thinking, speaking, and

listening – are physically demanding activities. "I was on the debate team in high school. I also played basketball. I was able to run up and down the court all day long. I reached the finals of my first debate tournament and had a series of three debates. After I finished I could hardly move. I climbed into an old yellow school bus, fell asleep, and didn't wake up until I reached home. That was strange for me. If you're really concentrating, critical listening is a physically exhausting experience. Listening as an audience member is more draining than we give it credit for.[28]

Peter Coughter warned, "The audience does not care about how much we know. The audience cares about how interesting what we tell them about what we know is."[29]

It can be daunting for us as speakers to cut our messages down to a more palatable length. But it's not much of a challenge for the team. If I wonder what to exclude, I just ask my teaching team. They can instantly (and sometimes brutally) identify what didn't fit, what distracted from it, and what isn't necessary.

While eighteen minutes might be most effective for a Ted Talk-style presentation as opposed to a Sunday sermon, the main point is that we tend to be better preachers when we go shorter rather than longer. Most preachers might

---

28 Carmine Gallo, *Talk like TED: The 9 Public Speaking Secrets of the World's Top Minds* (London: Pan Books, 2017), 185.

29 Peter Coughter, *Art of the Pitch - Persuasion and Presentation Skills That Win Business* (Palgrave Macmillan, 2012), Kindle Edition, 28.

teach forty minutes when they might be more effective at twenty-five or thirty minutes.

What does a teaching team look like? It looks like an environment of maximizing hard work.

Is it possible to prepare too much?

One question that keeps coming up at our preaching cohorts lately is: "Can a preacher prepare too much?"

I must admit there was a season in my preaching life when every Friday and Saturday night would find me in my office scrambling and searching for just the right joke, story, or quote to add to the Sunday sermon. And as I look back on those messages, they would have been better without my late-night tinkering. More often than not, I added the unnecessary.

I had a long-time associate who put at least forty hours into each of his messages, yet he was typically frustrated by not being able to pare down the message to a clear point or respect the time constraints of the Sunday service.

Dave Strobolakos from Grace Church in Henderson, Nevada, strives for what he calls the "Minimum Effective Dosage" (MED) in his message preparation. The MED is a medical term for an amount of a drug that is enough to cause positive changes. Many preachers flirt with the Maximum Tolerated Dosage (MTD) instead. We must recognize that there is a line between effectiveness and toxicity.

There is something incredibly freeing about having the team sign off that a presentation is ready to go.

A great way for a preacher to guard against over-dosing on sermon-prep is to run the talk by the teaching team. The team can declare that the message is ready or give clear suggestions as to what additions or subtractions need to be made. There is something incredibly freeing about having the team sign off that a presentation is ready to go. Get a team and allow them to say, "Enough."

MINI-CASE-STUDY:
THE BLOCK CHURCH, PHILADELPHIA, PENNSYLVANIA

The Block Church is a growing ministry seeking to revive Philly one block at a time. Lead Pastor, Joey Furjanic explains, "We definitely use 'team' for rest [giving the lead pastor time off], leadership development, training, and other perspectives."

The church has six speakers on rotation, the location pastors, two evangelists involved in the church, and five to ten people in training to speak. "My location pastors speak once a month," Furjanic says. "I write the sermons. They use the notes I create and add their own illustrations. We have five services, and some weekends we'll have five or ten different speakers, where younger or newer preachers I'm training will tag team. I usually do the introduction and close, but they preach the message."

Furjanic still does most of the preaching, but location pastors and other team members are growing into speaking more. Joey asks, "Who am I training? Who has influence? Who has potential? Who is gifted?" as he seeks to develop leaders. His bottom line for training is simple, "Watch me. And be open to feedback."

"If there's an overly strong main communicator," Furjanic cautions, "the drop off can be significant and people don't always want to come to church or be engaged when they know the main communicator isn't teaching. We experience some of this, but I cast vision constantly for the importance of hearing from others and how this develops maturity."

THE BIG CHALLENGE:

Gather your team to discuss an upcoming message. Focus the discussion on the following prompts: Is there a central passage that provides the main point of the message? What can be eliminated to make the message more effective? What still needs more work?

CHAPTER 7

AN OVERLOOKED SECRET

Our chief want is someone who will inspire us to be what we know we could be.

—Ralph Waldo Emerson

My greatest fear in life is that no-one will remember me after I'm dead.

—Some dead guy

I believe everyone has potential to become a world-class communicator and preacher.

—Dave Snyder, *The Laws of Communication for Preaching*

My wife, Lori, strolled to the car with our five-year-old grandson. "Jonah," she asked, "how much do you think I love you?" Jonah replied immediately and matter-of-factly, "More than a hundred."

Everyone wants to be loved, "More than a hundred."

Maybe you are like Lori. Perhaps you are gifted at making people feel loved more than a hundred.

The expansion of the early church was ignited in a big way by the gift and environment of encouragement – embodied by Barnabas.

> "Joseph, a Levite from Cyprus, whom the apos-
> tles called Barnabas (which means Son of

Encouragement), sold a field he owned and brought
the money and put it at the apostles' feet."

Acts 4:36-37 (NIV)

Barnabas' nickname highlighted his encouraging attitude. His generosity and uplifting spirit helped launch the
church and change the world.

But maybe you're not especially gifted at encouraging
people.

It seems reasonably obvious that the Apostle Paul did
not have an encouragement gift. He had an apostolic gift,
a preaching gift, a gift for getting things started. But he
doesn't appear to be a natural encourager.

Only once before Acts chapter 15 do we see Paul encouraging anyone. And that was when he was with Barnabas:

> After preaching the Good News in Derbe and mak
> ing many disciples, Paul and Barnabas returned to
> Lystra, Iconium, and Antioch of Pisidia, where they
> strengthened the believers. They encouraged them to
> continue in the faith, reminding them that we must
> suffer many hardships to enter the Kingdom of God.
>
> Acts 14:21-22 (NLT)

The big disagreement at the end of chapter 15 seems to
have had something to do with the encouragement issue.
Barnabas wanted to sponsor John Mark, Paul not so much.

> After some time, Paul said to Barnabas, "Let's go back
> and visit each city where we previously preached the

word of the Lord, to see how the new believers are
doing." Barnabas agreed and wanted to take along
John Mark. But Paul disagreed strongly, since John
Mark had deserted them in Pamphylia and had not
continued with them in their work. Their disagreement was so sharp that they separated.

Acts 15:36-39 (NLT)

Paul was not Mr. Encouragement like Barnabas. Paul
was Mr. Get-Things-Done, Mr. Public-Speaker, and even
Mr. Start-A-Riot. But we do see a slight shift in Paul's ministry after that encounter. Paul seems to add encouraging
others into his ministry tool-belt:

When Paul and Silas left the prison, they returned
to the home of Lydia. There they met with the
believers and encouraged them once more. Then
they left town.

Acts 16:40 (NLT)

When the uproar was over, Paul sent for the believers and encouraged them. Then he said good-bye
and left for Macedonia. While there, he encouraged
the believers in all the towns he passed through.

Acts 20:1-2 (NLT)

Watch out! Remember the three years I was with
you – my constant watch and care over you night
and day, and my many tears for you.

Acts 20:31 (NLT)

Just as day was dawning, Paul urged everyone to eat. "You have been so worried that you haven't touched food for two weeks," he said. "Please eat something now for your own good. For not a hair of your heads will perish... Then everyone was encouraged and began to eat."

Acts 27:33-34 & 36 (NLT)

If you have the gift of encouragement, you probably don't need a lesson or even encouragement to encourage others. It is part of who you are, and it will be a natural part of any teaching team you lead or join.

If you have the encouragement gene, then developing a teaching team is perfect for you. You will be a natural at it. You will love seeing, as Bob Buford used to say, "Your fruit grow on other people's trees." You will take Dave Ferguson's "ICNU" (I See in You) challenge to point out the great potential you easily see in others. You will be able to make a team concept thrive.

> **You will love seeing "your fruit grow on other people's trees."**

But if you are more like Paul than Barnabas, if you don't have a knack for encouraging others, don't get discouraged. You can still be effective fostering a teaching team.

My wife tells me regularly that a huge key to our teaching teams' effectiveness is my encouragement for, and belief in, the teachers. She says this is the overlooked piece to why we've been fruitful.

It is strange she would say something like that because I struggle with encouraging. I'm naturally quiet. I don't like to "pump sunshine" and I'm very wary of flattery, so I'm careful with compliments. Intentionally lifting up other people does not come naturally for me.

But that deficiency can actually turn into an advantage.

Have you heard of RBF? This stands for "Resting B---- Face." The term came from some 2013 movie I never saw, and Wikipedia describes it as: "A facial expression which unintentionally appears as if a person is angry, annoyed, irritated, or contemptuous, particularly when the individual is relaxed, resting, or not expressing any emotion." Other more gender-neutral phrases can be "Hostile Resting Face," or "Resting Murder Face."

I may or may not possess "Resting SOB Face," but I must admit, I am pretty sure I exhibit "Resting I-don't-think-that-guy-likes-me Face."

I can't tell you the number of times in my life people have asked if I was mad, sad, angry, or upset when I was actually pretty emotionless. I've tried feebly to mitigate this problem, but it is even more annoying when people say, "Stop with the fake smile," or, "What's with that stupid look on your face?"

Abraham Lincoln quipped, "Every man over forty is responsible for his face." I can only take solace that I don't look quite as dour as Abe.

But RBF can actually be something positive. Not having the gift of encouragement can be a plus. Here is how: When I say something encouraging, people know I really mean it!

Our teaching team folks – or at least most of them – know I care about them and are for them because they know I'm not one to give away empty compliments. I believe in the people on our teams!

I think of the boy who came home from little league practice with a big smile on his face. "How did practice go?" his mom asked. "I struck out every time," he said, "but it was a great practice." "Why is that?" his mother inquired. "Because," he explained, "the coach says I'm the best of the worst three!"

Top Ten Least Inspirational Things for a Coach to Say at Halftime

10. "If you don't mind, I'm going to leave early to beat the traffic."
9. "They may have the talent, size, and athleticism, but we have the nice helmets."
8. "Who's winning?"
7. "Enough strategy. Let me tell you guys about my Amway products."
6. "Has anyone seen my copy of, 'Football for Dummies?'"
5. "The best offense is...not *our* offense."
4. "I say, fellows! Vigorously propel that spheroid in the direction of the other chaps' goal!"
3. "It's not over until, ah, who am I kidding? It's over."
2. "Now get out there and rest on your laurels."
1. "What do you mean there's two more quarters?"

An overlooked element to teaching teams is a spirit of encouragement nurtured by the team leader.

How do we get there? How can we encourage encouragement?

We see a few hints in the life of the Apostle Paul.

Take courage

> That night the Lord appeared to Paul and said, "Be
> encouraged, Paul. Just as you have been a witness
> to me here in Jerusalem, you must preach the Good
> News in Rome as well."
>
> Acts 23:11 (NLT)

When Paul was in the midst of stormy waters, he spent
time with God and received great encouragement from his
heavenly father.

Let's get with God. Maybe he will actually appear to us
and tell us to be encouraged. Or maybe we will see in his
words that he always comes through, the end of the story
is…God wins, if we are on his side, we win too. There is
much to be encouraged about.

Get around encouragers

Perhaps God will encourage us through other people.
Intentionally spend more time with the Barnabas or the
Silas in your life.

Paul had a distinct advantage of having Barnabas take
him under his wing. That positivity helped propel Paul to
greatness.

A young man, hired by a supermarket, reported for his
first day of work. The manager greeted him with a warm
handshake and a smile, gave
him a broom, and said, "Your
first job will be to sweep out
the store." "But I'm a college

**An overlooked element to
teaching teams is a spirit of
encouragement nurtured
by the team leader.**

graduate," the young man replied indignantly. "Oh, I'm sorry. I didn't know that," said the manager. "Here, give me the broom, I'll show you how."

When Paul and Barnabas split, Paul immediately chose Silas. I suspect Silas was someone who possessed an encouragement gift. When we see Silas in action, we see him encouraging others.

> Then Judas and Silas, both being prophets, spoke at length to the believers, encouraging and strengthening their faith.
>
> Acts 15:32 (NLT)

> Around midnight Paul and Silas were praying and singing hymns to God, and the other prisoners were listening.
>
> Acts 16:25 (NLT)

Singing songs in prison sounds like something someone with an encouragement gift would do. I blame Silas.

If we spend time with encouragers, we will get encouraged and learn to encourage. I've learned a ton from watching my wife inspire and nurture others. I've grown in encouraging by watching my good friends Brian Burman and Paul Mints and Mike Pate and Willie Nolte and many others push people toward growth.

Just do it.

Paul received encouragement from God and others, and then he went out and actually did it:

> But take courage! None of you will lose your lives,
> even though the ship will go down.
>
> Acts 27:22 (NLT)

> So take courage! For I believe God. It will be just
> as he said.
>
> Acts 27:25 (NLT)

Johann Wolfgang von Goethe wrote, "Knowing is not enough; we must apply. Willing is not enough; we must do."

Dave Snyder, in *The Laws of Communication for Preaching* tells this story:

> When the game of golf was being introduced to the United States a Scottish man was asked to demonstrate for President Ulysses Grant. The man showed the President the tee and stuck it in the ground. He showed him the ball and carefully placed it on the tee. Then the man took out his club and addressed the ball. He took a powerful swing and sent dirt flying all over the President's beard. There the ball sat, still on the tee. The man swung again and missed. After six attempts the President said, "There seems to be a fair amount of exercise in this game, but I fail to see the purpose of the ball."[30]

Knowing is not enough; we must apply. Willing is not enough; we must do.

---

30 Dave Snyder, *The Laws of Communication for Preaching* (BubbaBooks Publishing, 2018), Kindle Edition.

Don't be afraid to swing and miss a few times. Don't be shy about getting dirty. Keep believing in your team. Keep encouraging.

What does a teaching team look like? It looks like an environment of encouragement.

MINI-CASE STUDY:

AMAZING GRACE CHRISTIAN CHURCH

INDIANAPOLIS, INDIANA

Lead Pastor Preston Adams explains, "I cannot, nor should I, be the only one in the church preaching and teaching. Team teaching gives room for growth in others. It also helps me prevent burnout and allows for me to take time away for rest or outside preaching engagements. My team approach involves intentional leadership development based on spiritual gifts assessments and individual passions. For those called to the preaching and/or teaching ministry, I've developed a curriculum that includes how to prepare, research, and write sermons. I also spend time teaching and practicing proper protocols of speaking, in one's home church and in churches where one might be invited to preach or teach."

Amazing Grace currently has eight capable preachers. Preston does the bulk of the teaching, while the others speak once or twice per year.

Adams assesses the gifts, passion, and commitment to Christ and to the church for each of the speakers. He observes how they serve the people and the community.

"I steer away from people who only want the limelight or notoriety that comes with being the 'speaker of the hour.' I'm pretty good at assessing motives."

Adam's curriculum develops and nurtures preachers and teachers. He challenges students to write sermons and Bible lessons even when they don't have preaching assignments. The church employs special days in the church calendar (Holy Week, Maundy Thursday, Easter, etc.) as training moments also.

Preston describes one downside to his approach: "Turnover versus commitment long-term. I've trained a number of people who have not remained in our ministry. While I don't consider this a waste of my time, it would have been nice to still have a few of the better teachers around."

THE BIG CHALLENGE:

Make a personal goal to intentionally encourage each member of your teaching team this month. It can be formal (i.e. written notes) or informal (i.e. a passing comment), whichever suits your style better. Be sure to include specific details about what you appreciate about them.

PART THREE

WHO?

CHAPTER 8

FINDING GOOD PLAYERS

Give me a hundred preachers who fear nothing but sin and desire nothing but God, and I care not a straw whether they be clergymen or laymen; such alone will shake the gates of hell and set up the kingdom of heaven on earth.

—John Wesley

You don't find leaders. You develop leaders.

—Craig Groeschel

There is nothing noble in being superior to your fellow man; true nobility is being superior to your former self.

—Ernest Hemingway

On April 16, 2000, the New England Patriots drafted Tom Brady as an extra quarterback out of the University of Michigan. It was the sixth round and Brady became the 199th pick of the draft. He was fourth string at the beginning of his rookie season. By his second season, he was second string, then Drew Bledsoe got hurt, and Brady was a starter. New England won the Super Bowl that year. Brady was named MVP. In terms of return on investment, it's probably the single greatest draft pick in the history of football: five Super Bowl rings, three Super Bowl MVPs, and more division titles than any quarterback in history. It's not even finished paying dividends. Brady may still have more seasons left in him.

All of the other NFL teams were kicking themselves that they missed their opportunity to choose Tom Brady, and they all did some soul searching as to what happened. You would think that the Patriots' front office would be ecstatic with how it turned out, and they were.

They were also disappointed – deeply so – in themselves. Brady's surprising abilities meant that the Patriots' scouting reports were way off. For all their evaluations of players, they'd somehow missed or miscalculated all of his intangible attributes. They'd let this gem wait until the sixth round. Someone else could have drafted him. On top of

The workers are few. But they are not extinct. Workers can be found, developed, and deployed.

that, they didn't even know they were right about Brady until injuries knocked out Bledsoe, their prized starter, and forced them to realize his potential. So, even though their bet paid off, the Patriots spent a great deal of time looking into what could have prevented the nature of the the pick from happening in the first place. Not that they were nit-picking or indulging in perfectionism. They wanted to raise their standards of evaluating talent.

For years, Scott Pioli, director of personnel for the Patriots, kept a photo on his desk of Dave Stachelski, a player the team had drafted in the fifth round, but who never made it through training camp. Pioli says, "It was a reminder: You don't have it all figured out. Stay focused. Do better."

How can we do a better job of finding good players? How do we find leaders or more preachers and teachers?

I lead a couple international church planting networks, and lately we've seen a strong upsurge in the number of churches we've started. The number one question I get from other ministry executives is, "Where do you find your leaders?" They want to know how we've succeeded with "recruiting" and where we find people to start churches.

There are similar questions that come when we mention our teaching team approach. "Great, but where do you find your teammates?"

Jesus put it this way:

> Then he said to his disciples, "The harvest is plentiful but the workers are few."
>
> Matthew 9:37 (NIV)

Jesus admitted that finding teammates is difficult. The workers are few.

A decade ago, when the church multi-site movement was emerging, many of us thought that finding a campus pastor would be a whole lot easier than finding lead pastors. I suspect many anticipated a potential glut of leaders vying to be campus pastors. It turns out that finding campus pastors isn't any easier than finding lead pastors, church planters, solid worship leaders, children's ministers, and teaching team members.

The workers are few. But they are not extinct. Workers can be found, developed, and deployed. We can expect finding leaders to be tough, but we can also expect to find leaders and teachers and preachers anyway.

Where do we find them?

Let's look at the Bible's Book of Acts, starting at the beginning of the narrative, for some ideas:

1. Release the apostles to find leaders

Then the apostles returned to Jerusalem…

Acts 1:12 (NIV)

The story of Acts is a story of leadership development. It is a history of finding teachers and leaders. If we are not careful, we might miss the implication that the apostolic types were the ones that did most of the leadership spotting.

For years I've entertained a theory that apostolic types are natural – or actually, super-natural – at garnering leaders. People with an apostolic gift tend to have a distinctive bent toward finding leaders.

The word apostle is most often used to refer to the original twelve who followed Jesus. Those would be the "Capital 'A' Apostles." The Greek word means "one who is sent out." It denotes the pioneering supporter of any new cause. A close Latin translation is "mission," from which we get the term missionary. There are leaders today whom we would consider "small 'a' apostles."

Alan Hirsch and Jeff Weber define it this way: "Apostles extend the gospel. As the 'sent ones,' they ensure that the faith is transmitted from one context to another and from one generation to the next. They are always thinking about the future, bridging barriers, establishing the church in new contexts, developing leaders, networking trans-locally."[31]

These apostolic types seem to be especially talented at consistently discovering potential leaders. Maybe it is because the apostles know they won't be around long, so they are always looking for someone who might want or warrant a handoff.

When I suspect someone has that small 'a' apostle gift, I typically see potential leaders all around them. If you ask an apostle, "Where do you find leaders?" they may hesitate to answer because discovering leaders is an easy task for them — it is simply who they are.

2. Look at who was been hanging around

> Therefore it is necessary to choose one of the men who have been with us the whole time the Lord Jesus was living among us…
>
> Acts 1:21 (NIV)

The early church leaders didn't immediately place an ad on churchstaffing.com or contact ZipRecruiter. They didn't hire an outside agency to deliver a truckload of resumes to the church. The first thing they did was to look immediately around their group.

Later, they made a similar move:

---

31 Alan Hirsch and Jeff Weber, "What Is APEST?" The Forgotten Ways, accessed November 22, 2018, http://www.theforgottenways.org/what-is-apest.aspx.

Then the apostles and elders, with the whole church, decided to choose some of their own men and send them to Antioch with Paul and Barnabas. They chose Judas (called Barsabbas) and Silas, men who were leaders among the believers.

Acts 15:22 (NIV)

When I was leading church planter assessments at Green Lake Conference Center in Green Lake, Wisconsin, Marlan Mincks would drive to our events from his home in Iowa to sit on the assessment team. Marlan was a brand new church planter at the time. He admitted that serving as an assessor was the best coaching he could ever receive, so he came to just about every single assessment center we offered.

Marlan often joked that when he came through our assessment looking to be the lead guy, my first question to him was, "Have you ever thought about becoming a number two guy?" I don't remember that interaction, but I do remember Marlan being a quiet person, an introvert who seemed to be taking in everything.

When I left that church planting group there was one person I recommended to replace me as a leader – Marlan Mincks. And he has proven to be an excellent leader. Often the ones who are the best leaders are right in front of us.

Years ago, our church did a nationwide search for a new youth pastor. We brought in people from all over the country only to be extremely disappointed with the resumes, interviews, and results we saw and experienced. Finally, one of the leaders in our church asked, "Why are we conducting a nationwide search when we already have

the best candidate right here in our church?" He was refer-
ring to my son, Tim.

I admit I was probably overcompensating in an effort
to avoid nepotism. Our leadership team was most likely
suffering from at least a tad bit of "prophet-without-honor
syndrome."

> Jesus told them, "A prophet is honored everywhere
> except in his own hometown and among his rela-
> tives and his own family."
>
> Mark 6:4 (NLT)

Tim had been with the church from the very beginning. He served on the set-up team before there was even
a set-up team. He was right in front of us, and we almost
missed him. Not only did he serve admirably as youth
pastor in that church, he is now the Lead Pastor.

Often the best person for that special seat on the bus is
already on the bus.

Our teaching teams at the Journey Church in Elk
Grove, California, are made up of people who have been
part of the church. We haven't felt any need to go outside the church because we've discovered that more than a
dozen folks inside the church have teaching and preaching
potential.

3. Ask the entire group for suggestions

> So the Twelve gathered all the disciples together
> and said, "...Brothers and sisters, choose seven men

from among you who are known to be full of the
Spirit and wisdom."

Acts 6:2-3 (NIV)

A few chapters in to the Book of Acts, the church faced
a critical need for more leaders. So they asked everyone in
the fellowship for input.

There is merit in asking everyone to be a spotter, and to
call for nominations.

A key to finding good leaders is to get the word out
that we are looking for more leaders. This means developing an ongoing multiplication mindset.

When we went to a teaching team approach, people
assumed we were always looking for teachers, and often
unsolicited, we get lots of leads.

4. Allow the encouragers to find leaders

But Barnabas took him and brought him to the
apostles.

Acts 9:27 (NIV)

News of this reached the church in Jerusalem, and
they sent Barnabas to Antioch.

Acts 11:22 (NIV)

Barnabas went to Tarsus to look for Saul, and when
he found him, he brought him to Antioch.

Acts 11:25 (NIV)

I've had a theory going for many years that encouragers, as well as apostles, locate leaders fairly easily. Encouragers tend to see the potential in people.

I asked Ralph Moore once if he had the gift of encouragement. He seemed surprised. "You are never lacking leaders around you. I bet you see a leadership component in everyone," I remarked. Ralph explained why he was startled: "I never really knew what my primary spiritual gift was, but recently a woman in our church told me it is so obvious. 'You're an encourager!' she claimed. Maybe I am," he admitted.

> **The Holy Spirit actually spoke to the church about leaders. Many of us would love for that to happen to us. Maybe it has, but we weren't listening.**

Encouragers encourage everyone! They instinctively know how to find teachers and leaders.

5. Listen to the Holy Spirit

The Holy Spirit said…

Acts 13:2 (NIV)

The Holy Spirit actually spoke to the church about leaders. Many of us would love for that to happen to us. Maybe it has, but we weren't listening.

In Acts 15 the apostles and the elders mention this in a letter:

For it seemed good to the Holy Spirit and to us…

Acts 15:8 (NLT)

The Holy Spirit does speak.

As I was working on this, a thought popped into my mind about a couple in our church who may become church planters one day. Where did that thought come from? Maybe it came from the Holy Spirit.

Dan Southerland says many of us are good at thanking, worshiping, and even asking God, but how many of us pause to even listen to what God is saying.

Luke's account of one of Jesus' statements goes this way:

> He told them, "The harvest is plentiful, but the workers are few. Ask the Lord of the harvest, therefore, to send out workers into his harvest field."
>
> Luke 10:2 (NIV)

Prayer is Jesus' primary tip for finding leaders, and I suspect preachers too.

> Then they all prayed, "O Lord, you know every heart. Show us which of these men you have chosen..."
>
> Acts 1:24 (NLT)

In an examination paper, a professor wanted students to sign a form stating that they had not received any outside assistance. Unsure of whether he should sign the form, a student stated that he had prayed for the assistance of God. The professor carefully studied the answer script and then said, "You can sign it with a clear conscience. God did not assist you."

But he does assist us in finding team members.

Let's pray them in. I didn't actually start seeing potential teachers show up until I started praying for them.

> They all joined together constantly in prayer.
>
> Acts 1:14 (NIV)

Fasting while we pray seems to be part of the strategy as well.

> Paul and Barnabas chose some leaders for each of the churches. Then they went without eating and prayed that the Lord would take good care of these leaders.
>
> Acts 14:23 (CEV)

6. Look at Denomination and Network Leaders

The early church found some of their leaders and speakers at a network leaders' gathering in Jerusalem.

> Then the apostles and elders together with the whole church in Jerusalem chose delegates, and they sent them to Antioch of Syria with Paul and Barnabas to report on this decision. The men chosen were two of the church leaders – Judas (also called Barsabbas) and Silas.
>
> Acts 15:22 (NLT)

One of the reasons why I hesitated – for years – to move into full-time, second-level ministry is a disturbing trend I observed among denominational leaders. One of the roughest parts of denominational work appears to be finding a suitable local church in which to call home. Over the years, I have seen the denominational workers struggle with this. But more than that, their spouses and children struggled even more.

Judicatory workers feel a need to be in a different church every weekend in order to serve their constituents, but this leaves their family stranded. Sure, some jump right into a church and get involved. But I have seen far too many others disconnect, drop out, and even question their faith.

I did not want that to happen to me or my family. My wife did not need to leave the church we started – and neither did I – when I stepped out of the pastorate.

A friend told me recently, "Well, staying involved in a church was easy for you. Your son is the pastor." I wanted to say, "Yeah, easy, it only took me two decades to raise him, and another decade for him to be trained in ministry. In the meantime, I did an exhaustive search for years working to hand off the church I planted – so, yeah, right, it was easy." That's what I wanted to say. Instead, I didn't say anything, I just smirked.

Most denominational leaders have some sort of speaking gift, and many are very good at it. Why don't we look to them to be on our teaching teams?

7. Find people you want to hang out with

> Paul came to... Lystra, where a disciple named
> Timothy lived... The believers at Lystra and

Iconium spoke well of him. Paul wanted to take
him along on the journey, so he circumcised him…

Acts 16:1-3 (NIV)

Here is one approach to finding leaders and speakers:
look for someone who is well-liked, someone you enjoy
being around, and then circumcise him! Actually, ignore
that last part. But do look for likeable people.

Peter Coughter encourages this mindset in his book,
*The Art of the Pitch: Persuasion and Presentation Skills that
Win Business*:

> In great presentations, teams present as if they really
> like one another. Even if you don't, find a way to at
> least seem like you do. Clients can smell it a mile
> away if you don't get along, and they will dismiss
> you immediately if they sense it.[32]

CASE STUDY:

COLD SPRINGS CHURCH, PLACERVILLE, CALIFORNIA

Pastor David Cooke wants to equip people to express
and use their giftedness as fully as possible. Asked why
he employs a team approach to teaching, Cooke says,
"Primarily it is to more fully embrace the priesthood of
all believers - God has called all to serve, not just the

---

32 Coughter, *Art of the Pitch*

vocational leaders. As well, it is important and valuable to hear different 'voices' to help us see things from different perspectives – whether that be generational, gender, etc. It is also unhealthy for someone to teach fifty-two times each year! We have three services per week and it is a real toll to preach that much. Having rest creates greater creativity, energy, and passion for when you are preaching/teaching. Preaching/teaching is something you can only improve at by actually doing it. The only way we can have more and better teachers is to give them real opportunities to teach."

Cold Springs has seven active speakers right now. Four others are in the pipeline. Cooke gives teachers the opportunity to practice their gift "live," primarily in the contexts outside of Sunday morning worship such as retreats, guys and ladies breakfasts, youth gatherings, and equipping events.

With thriving youth, men's and women's ministries, the church teaching team is both need-based and fulfills the leadership development value of the church's vision.

David cites these advantages of a team approach:

1. It is being obedient to scripture to develop and equip others.
2. It is good stewardship.
3. It creates a healthier rhythm of ministry for the primary teacher so there are seasons of rest.
4. It creates less dependence upon one person and helps guard against the cult of personality.
5. It gives opportunity for new voices to be heard and shared.

6. It creates a proper humility for the primary teacher that, yes, the church can exist without their voice being front and center all of the time.

He also sees these downsides of a teaching team:

1. The quality and skill level can vary greatly.
2. People can want "the professional" to do it so they get restless.
3. You have to give up control as a leader. (I think this is actually an advantage, but others may not see it that way.)
4. They might like someone better than you! (And then you have to kick them out of the church so you can keep your power and control!)
5. Recent research by Gallup shows that the quality of preaching is still extremely important, if not the most important thing, for adults coming to church. I have found this true with older youth, as well, in regard to the level of communication of youth leaders. (Almost) everyone is bad when they start.

THE BIG CHALLENGE:

It's time! Compile a list of people that you will invite to be developed on your teaching team. Consider those with whom you enjoy hanging out. Consult with the Holy Spirit, your leadership team, and other trusted advisors for potential members of the team. The list need not be exhaustive nor perfected yet. Just get some names down and start inviting!

CHAPTER 9

THE BENCH

Though Steve Young had been the star of his high school football team and was heavily recruited by colleges across the country, he entered Brigham Young University as their eighth-string quarterback. Since seven other quarterbacks stood between Steve and playing time, his coach relegated him to the "hamburger squad" - a unit composed of the least valuable players whose primary role was to run plays so the BYU defensive line could practice.

—Angela Duckworth, "Grit:
The Power or Passion and Perseverance

During the first Sunday in February, I did what many, if not most, Americans do on the first Sunday in February: I watched the Super Bowl. This year Nick Foles quarterbacked an almost flawless game and his Philadelphia Eagles beat the New England Patriots. Remarkably, just several weeks before the big game, Nick Foles found himself on the bench. Carson Wentz was the Eagle's starting quarterback, but he was injured in mid-December and deemed unable to play for the rest of the season. So Foles came off the bench and surprised everyone.

Maybe it should not have been such a surprise. After all, Foles' opposing quarterback, Tom Brady, started his illustrious "Greatest of All Time" NFL career on the bench.

He wasn't put into the lineup until the starting QB, Drew Bledsoe, had a season-ending injury.

I suspect that there are amazing players on everyone's bench – even your church's. Actually, this is more than a hunch: I predict that there are incredibly talented players on your organization's bench.

Just a few days ago, I met with several folks from our church for our teaching training time. As is our custom, we had scheduled two people each to give a ten-minute presentation. One of them stood up and astonished us with her skill. She was clear, she had a prop that actually worked well, she made a great point, she got us to rethink a familiar biblical story, she engaged, and she finished under the ten-minute time table. Our team sat silently; it was a jaw-dropping speech.

> **If we are not careful, we can completely miss the incredibly talented players on our teams, and even on our bench.**

"How many times have you given that talk before?" I asked. It was so good that it had to be something she's worked on for years. "This is the first time," she explained. "I started working on it a few weeks ago for this meeting."

Stupidly, I was stunned. Stupidly – because there are incredibly talented people on your team and on ours. I should have anticipated it.

Pastors can easily slip into becoming like Jeff Fisher. Fisher was a long-time football coach in the NFL. He holds the record for the most losses as a head coach – 165 in the regular season. He had to be good enough to stick around so long and lose that many games. (He actually won 173!) In Fisher's last two seasons he had three quarterbacks: Nick Foles – Fisher cut him, then he became the Most Valuable Player of the Super Bowl; Case Keenam – Fisher benched him, then Keenam led his new team to the NFC Championship game; and Jared Goff – Fisher got zero wins out of Goff, who then became the NFL's most-improved player under a new coach.

If we are not careful, we can completely miss the incredibly talented players on our teams, and even on our bench.

Recently I was with a group of church planting leaders for some meetings in Houston, Texas. The facilitators brought in a retired woman, a former business leader, to speak to us. She came down off the stage and worked the crowd like an exceptional comedian, politician, and motivational speaker all rolled into one. It was an amazing display of encouragement and verbal talent. After her talk there was a short time available for questions and answers. One of the first questions was, "Wow, you are a great communicator. Do you speak regularly at your church?" That question seemed to shake this woman. She paused, leaned over and whispered, "Oh, no, my pastor doesn't know about my speaking ability. He would never have me on stage at church. My role is to be a greeter – once a month."

Again, I was stunned. There are incredibly talented people on the bench in your organization or church.

Then Todd Wilson took the stage and made this observation: "In every church there are talented people, and their pastor has no idea what to do with them."

Have you ever noticed how the disciples of Jesus solved problems in the Bible's Book of Acts? For sure, they always prayed. Prayer was a given. And they often asked for a miracle in their prayers.

But there is another solution they typically went to next: The Bench. Many of the early churches dilemmas were solved with the bench.

Judas betrayed Jesus and his team. What do you do with a problem like that? The Apostles went to the bench.

The widows were not getting enough food. What do you do with a problem like that? The Apostles went to the bench. They chose men like Stephen and Phillip.

> Stephen, a man full of God's grace and power, performed amazing miracles and signs among the people.
>
> Acts 6:8 (NLT)

Stephen wasn't even on the leadership team, he was on the bench. The first martyr in the Christian Church came off the bench.

Philip opened the doors for Christianity to spread in Samaria and Ethiopia.

> Philip, for example, went to the city of Samaria and told the people there about the Messiah. Crowds listened intently to Philip because they were eager to hear his message and see the miraculous signs he did. Many evil spirits were cast out, screaming as they left their victims. And many who had been

paralyzed or lame were healed. So there was great joy in that city.

Acts 8:5-8 (NLT)

In Acts chapter 15, Paul and Barnabas have a disagreement about the bench. The dispute becomes so charged that they part ways. What do you do with a problem like that? Paul and Barnabas went to the bench.

Barnabas took John Mark with him and sailed for Cyprus. Paul chose Silas, and as he left, the believers entrusted him to the Lord's gracious care. Then he traveled throughout Syria and Cilicia, strengthening the churches there.

Acts 15:40-41 (NLT)

Mark and Silas turned out to be two pretty good players. There were incredibly talented people on the early church's bench.

The early church solved betrayal issues, discord problems, and relational struggles with the bench. I suspect we can too.

MINI-CASE-STUDY:
CALVARY LIGHTHOUSE UNITED, DAVIE, FLORIDA

Lead Pastor Eric Gamero has recruited five other pastors who teach. As lead communicator, Gamero gives direction and vision for the teaching calendar and preaches about

75% of the weekly teaching. The lead communicator typically kicks-off and closes a series.

Eric says, "Each of the six communicators have different personalities, life experiences, and teaching styles. Being a multi-cultural and multi-generational church, the benefit of having a teaching team allows for each teacher to get constructive feedback and a different perspective on the message they are planning to communicate. Practically, this allows for the main communicator to get a weekend off each month to pray, plan, and prepare for the future, while allowing the other teachers multiple weeks to hone and perfect their message."

The lead communicator speaks between thirty-six to forty times a year. One other pastor speaks three to five times a year. Each other pastor speaks one to two times a year, and we allow two to three times a year for a guest communicator.

Here is the training approach: "For the teachers with less experience, I make sure to sit with them through the entire process of concept to completion of the teaching. I'll tell them how I would teach the text, give them my examples, but then allow them to make the message their own. Specific results happen by design, not desire – so, if I want a single message be cohesive to the entire series, as lead communicator, I have to hold the teacher's hand and lead them. For the more experienced teachers, I give them the main points that I feel need to be communicated and allow them to build around it themselves. After they teach, I personally offer constructive feedback. When I teach, I allow the teaching team to hear my message in its entirety most

Thursdays before I share and walk them through why I said things the way I did, and what I'm hoping to accomplish from the teaching."

The benefits of a team are the church hears from multiple teachers, not one. This creates a culture that places higher value on God's word rather than God's messengers. The main communicator gets needed rest to prevent burnout and the burden of having to always have a message prepared. If a communicator gets sick, there's always someone else who can jump in immediately. It also sets up the church for future success beyond the influence of one main communicator.

A downside to the team approach is that people like predictability. When their favorite teacher is not teaching, it can lead to disappointment. Some people are attracted to a personality before they are attracted to the ministry of a church.

THE BIG CHALLENGE:

Create a systematic way to involve and train new people on your teaching team, even if they admittedly might not currently be ready to speak on a Sunday. Consider it a lower-risk entry point that could serve as a reserve and an extra source of encouragement for the teaching team.

Need a coach to help you?

Contact *www.ExcelNetwork.org/Next-Steps*

CHAPTER 10

A WORD ABOUT WOMEN

*If you don't want women breaking down the doors, simply
open them for them.*

—Hannah Anderson

*I am a laugher. I can take jokes and make jokes. I know
good fun when I'm having it and I also know when I'm
being dismissed and ridiculed. I was the elephant in the
room with a skirt on.*

—Beth Moore

*Many women have received power through the grace of
God and have performed many deeds of manly valor.*

—Clement of Alexandria

D r. William Thomas was once asked the question, "How do you handle women in the church." Thomas replied, "In a word, don't!"

I hesitated to write about preaching. I hesitated even more to bring up the topic of women preachers. Should women be pastors? Should women be preaching in our churches?

I used to have this all figured out. I remember knowing all the answers on this topic. That was a long time ago. I don't have many answers anymore.

I work with some denominations and networks that embrace women as Lead Pastors, and I work with some groups that don't support women as pastors. Both groups typically have about the same number of women pastors!

One friend who leads a church planting network for her denomination admitted to me that she found it incredibly difficult to lead a church as a woman. "The only jobs I could ever get were the ones that even the least skilled of the men wouldn't take."

Another woman preacher, Anna Garlin Spencer, was asked if she faced any special obstacles as a woman in the ministry. "Only one," she answered, "The lack of a pastor's wife."

My daughter, Tricia, is a missionary overseas – part of a mission organization where women are in the majority – which is true of pretty much all mission groups. She has been compelled to do the teaching for many of the Sunday services she has attended. She'd rather not lead. She'd rather not teach. Actually, it is stronger than a rather not. Tricia she says really truly does not want to teach, but someone has to do it. This whole topic is muddy.

> **God is being purposely ambiguous about some issues. That's okay. The bottom line is to love each other.**

Back in the 1980s in Denver, Colorado, I heard Elisabeth Elliot give an amazing sermon on why women should never be allowed to preach. I left that venue perplexed and bewildered.

I'm still a bit baffled. That's not surprising, because the Bible could be clearer. I've heard the arguments on both sides, and I will not attempt to convince you one way or another.

Paul wrote a letter discussing our different gifts and roles. Sandwiched in between two chapters on the topic is the great chapter on love. Paul says if you don't have love, you don't have anything. He also says, "Now we see things imperfectly, like puzzling reflections in a mirror, but then we will see everything with perfect clarity" (1 Corinthians 13:12, NLT).

God is being purposely ambiguous about some issues. That's okay. The bottom line is to love each other.

But I do want to convince you to consider having women on your teaching team. Before you label me a heretic or assume I am on your side, please hear me out.

Having women on your teaching team doesn't necessarily mean you have women preach in your church. Whether you are complementarian, egalitarian, complegalitarian, vegetarian, or not much of an "arian" at all, let me encourage you to invite women onto your team.

There are several reasons why having women on your teaching team is a must:

1. Women have speaking gifts.

> Leaving the next day, we reached Caesarea and stayed at the house of Philip the evangelist, one of the Seven. He had four unmarried daughters who prophesied.
>
> Acts 21:8-9 (NIV)

> When the day of Pentecost came, they were all together in one place. Suddenly a sound like the blowing of a violent wind came from heaven and

filled the whole house where they were sitting. They saw what seemed to be tongues of fire that separated and came to rest on each of them. All of them were filled with the Holy Spirit...

Acts 2:1-4 (NIV)

"Your sons and daughters will prophesy..."

Acts 2:17 (NIV)

Women are given spiritual gifts, and some women have been given gifts for speaking.

2. Women need to be trained in speaking.

When Priscilla and Aquila heard him, they invited him to their home and explained to him the way of God more adequately.

Acts 18:26 (NIV)

Priscilla was a woman who was involved in training for teaching. Actually, she was on the faculty, doing at least part of the training.

One of the reasons we have women on our teaching teams is women need to be trained to be better teachers.

If we are looking for a speaker for a men's breakfast, retreat, or event, we are inundated with possibilities. But if we are looking for a woman to speak at a women's event, let's face it, the options are few.

Denominations that encourage women preachers generally like to have a least one woman speak at their

denominational meetings. I have sat through my share –
and your share – of these gatherings. The male speakers tend to be great. The women speakers can tend to be,
well…not always that great.

Have I offended everyone yet?

Offended or not, doesn't it make sense to help women
get better at speaking? Exactly how else will they improve?

Beth Moore admits, "Some will inevitably argue that
the disrespect was not over gender but over my lack of formal education, but that, too, largely goes back to issues
of gender. Where was a woman in my generation and
denomination to get seminary training to actually teach
the Scriptures?"[33]

It's bad enough that most men preachers never take
another preaching course after Bible school or seminary,
what's worse is we don't even encourage women to take
those courses.

Hannah Anderson says, "If Paul is correct that the
church is 'the pillar and ground of truth,' the way forward
is not to shame female leaders for using their gifts without
theological credentials, the way forward is for the church
to identify and support gifted women, partnering with
them via theological training and commissioned ministry
positions.

Women need to be trained for teaching teams too.
I asked a friend of mine, who is a woman and a Senior
Pastor, if she would allow me to use her church in one of
the mini-case studies. Here is her reply:

33 Beth Moore, "A Letter to My Brothers," Living Proof Ministries Blog, May 31, 2018, accessed
November 22, 2018, https://blog.lproof.org/2018/05/a-letter-to-my-brothers.html.

Thank you for thinking of me and our church. However, I do not think ours is qualified to be a team teaching church. We have three congregations and a pastor to lead each congregation. I will be preaching in all three sometimes. I am afraid we are not the church that you want to use as an example in your book.

3. Women see some things that men don't see

A police man is driving up a steep, narrow mountain road. A woman is driving down the same road. As they pass each other, the woman leans out of the window and yells "Pig! Pig! Pig!" The cop is taken aback. He leans out of his window and replies, "Witch!" Then the cop rounds the next corner and crashes into a pig.

We call Mary Beth, one of the women on our church's teaching team, our "canary in the coal mine." Miners used to carry caged canary birds down into their coal mines. If dangerous gases like carbon monoxide or methane accumulated, the gases would kill the canaries first. This signaled to the miners to get out of the mine quickly. The idiom now refers to someone – or something – who, due to her or his or its sensitivity to the surroundings, acts as an early warning of possible adverse conditions or danger.

If half of our congregation is made up of women, we might actually do a better job of preaching if we asked some women for input.

Mary Beth sits through our pre-service run through of the sermon every week. She is quick to tell us what may be a sensitive illustration, joke, or quip. We need her on our team.

If half of our congregation is made up of women, and it is usually more than half, we might actually do a better job of preaching if we asked some women for input.

4. Women can address some topics better than men.

> The king rose, and with him the governor and Bernice and those sitting with them. After they left the room, they began saying to one another, "This man is not doing anything that deserves death or imprisonment."
>
> Acts 26:30 (NIV)

King Agrippa II had a sister named Bernice, and evidently, he valued her opinion.

I am so tired of speaking about mothers on Mother's Day. What do I know about it? I know I want to honor my Mom, and my wife, but beyond that, I'm not qualified.

A couple years ago, I approached two women on our team and asked if they would speak on Mother's Day. Immediately, both of them replied – at the same time: "I hate Mother's Day!"

"Doesn't every Mom love Mother's Day?" I thought. Then I asked, "Why is that?" I'd give you their answers, but it would be better if you asked a mom yourself. Some things are best answered by mothers.

How about Mary? Ruth? Esther? Deborah? Lydia? How about Mary Magdalene? Labor pain? Childbirth? Exclusion? Injustice? There are numerous topics we need women to speak into – they have more insight and authority on them than most men. Women can actually speak into every topic!

Mary Beth Burrell quipped, "Proverbs 31 isn't the only passage in the Bible that applies to women!"

And Crystal Virtue said, "Christianity is the first religion that elevated women to equal standing and welcomes all people. 'I now realize how true it is that God does not show favoritism' (Acts 20:34). God wants us all to show respect, but He gave a voice to both men and women for the praise of His glory."

5. Women have been treated worse than they deserve.

It frustrates me when I sense the answer to injustice promoted as swinging the pendulum so far to the other side that we smack everyone else on the head with it. That's not at all what I am suggesting. I'm proposing that including women on your teaching team might be a big step in a muchneeded or even somewhat-needed attitude adjustment.

Beth Moore, in "A Letter to My Brothers," put it this way:

> I'm asking for your increased awareness of some of the skewed attitudes many of your sisters encounter. Many churches quick to teach submission are often slow to point out that women

were also among the followers of Christ (Luke 8), that the first recorded word out of His resurrected mouth was "woman" (John 20:15), and that same woman was the first evangelist. Many churches wholly devoted to teaching the household codes are slow to also point out the numerous women with whom the Apostle Paul served and for whom he possessed obvious esteem. We are fully capable of grappling with the tension the two spectrums create, and we must if we're truly devoted to the whole counsel of God's Word.[34]

Why is Junia (a clearly female name) listed as an apostle?

Say hello to Andronicus and Junia, my relatives and my fellow prisoners. They are prominent among the apostles, and they were in Christ before me.

Romans 16:7 (CEB)

Why was her name changed to Junias in 1927? Scot McKnight writes, "Junias is a man who didn't exist with a name that didn't exist in the ancient world."[35] And why was it changed back in 1929? As I said, I don't have all the answers.

Why is Priscilla mentioned first five out of the seven times she is named with her husband in the Scriptures? Here is my answer: I am not sure. Aquila is listed first twice. Maybe it's a "both-and" situation?

---

34   Beth Moore, "A Letter to My Brothers" https://blog.lproof.org/2018/05/a-letter-to-my-brothers.html.
35   Scot McKnight, *Junia Is Not Alone* (Patheos Press, 2011), Kindle Edition, Locations 93-94.

Greet Priscilla and Aquila, my co-workers in Christ
Jesus.

Acts 16:3 (NIV)

If women are truly co-workers, let's treat them like
co-workers. Include them on your team!

MINI-CASE-STUDY:

REBIRTH LA, LOS ANGELES, CALIFORNIA

Lé Selah Richardson says, "I believe team preaching offers
different communication styles that appeal to different audiences. It also attracts a new demographic to the
church. These things are important to help with the growth
of a church plant - especially taking into consideration that
I am a woman Lead Pastor and Church Planter."

Rebirth LA's preachers are enlisted from those who
have never sought out an opportunity to preach. They are
selected through a process of prayer, discernment, and
response from the Holy Spirit - based upon a basic criteria
of discipleship, study, and servanthood.

Rebirth LA's team preaching approach is in its infancy
phase and is executed through covenant relationships.
Four preachers are currently in training. None of them have
any formal theological training or teaching/preaching experience. Some have minimal public speaking experience. As
a result, covenant brotherhood/sisterhood relationships
and marriages help with support, trust, and confidence to
teach.

Lé writes, "I have found that pairing two accountability partners is far more effective than two individuals who have no existing relationship. For instance, the extroverted entertainer and the introverted music producer are showing great promise as a teaching team. Pairing a husband and wife team offers a holistic approach to the exegesis of text and bringing the sermon. In both scenarios, one is more of a preacher and the other is a teacher."

Selah believes, "The advantage of preaching teams is the tenacity of relationships between the team members. The teams are showing greater commitment to the great commission. Also, they tend to be a safety net for one another's shortfalls. The disadvantages are the human condition of competitiveness and comparison to one another's different gifts and graces. There are times when communication challenges and disputes can be easily discerned. Not to mention the complaints from church members when I brought forth this plan."

The preachers in training get their initial start by offering devotionals during weekly prayer calls and life groups. The next step is a preacher's boot camp designed by Lé to help with basic public speaking, teaching, and preaching techniques. The ultimate goal is the have the teams alternate every fourth Sunday. These goals are a work in progress.

THE BIG CHALLENGE:

If you haven't done so already, add some women to the list of invitees to your teaching team.

PART FOUR

HOW?

CHAPTER 11

TRAINING TIME

If thou thinkest twice, before thou speakest once, thou wilt speak twice the better for it.

—William Penn

The church is not a place to be entertained. It is a place to be equipped, enabled to go and do the mission of God.

—Sam Stephens

We are not God's gift to people, Jesus is.

—Jodi Hickerson

In the 1990s, Christian Motivational guru, Peter Lowe, held one of his "Get Motivated" seminars in San Francisco. One of the speakers was then-just-retired football hero, Joe Montana. Montana's talk was, at best, awkward. It was evident that Montana was quite uncomfortable giving a speech, especially to a large live audience. The crowd responded graciously…after all, he was a hometown hero.

When Peter Lowe's group came to Northern California the next year, I was surprised to see, once again, Joe Montana on the schedule. I braced myself for another uneasy presentation, only to be amazed by Montana's newfound oratory skills. The former quarterback looked as natural behind the lectern as he did behind his offensive line in his playing days. He was clear, poised, funny, and influential. I don't recall exactly what he said, but I do remember walking away realizing that much of public speaking can be taught.

There's an old, but effective story about a woman who went to see her lawyer because she was seeking a divorce. The lawyer asked, "Do you have any grounds?' "Yes," the woman replied, "we have about forty acres." "No, that's not what I meant," the lawyer said. "If you want a divorce you need some sort of suit." "Oh, I have several pant suits," the woman responded. "You don't understand," the lawyer persisted. "You need to have a reason for the divorce. Do you have some sort of a grudge?" "Not really," she said. "We just have a carport." "No, no, no," the lawyer went on. "Is there something one of you does that really annoys the other. For example, do you wake up grouchy?" "No," she said, "I usually just let him sleep." "Lady, you're driving me crazy." the exasperated lawyer said. "All I want to know is why you want a divorce." "Oh, that's simple," the woman said. "You see, my husband just doesn't know how to communicate."

> **As the leader, personally invite potential speakers or students to your training.**

How can we learn to communicate more effectively?

Earlier today, a church planter called and asked for ten minutes of my time. "I preached forty-something times last year and it just about killed me," he said. "One of my goals this year is to get a teaching team going. I've got a former pastor in my church, he has some good upfront skills, but there are a few things I'd like to work on with him before I unleash him on the congregation. But he is older than me…what do I do?"

Once you have identified potential speakers, what is the next step?

Here are some suggestions for training time:

1. Invitation Only

When starting a teaching team, or teaching training group, don't allow just anyone to attend. As the leader, personally invite potential speakers or students to your training.

> Paul went first to Derbe and then to Lystra, where there was a young disciple named Timothy. His mother was a Jewish believer, but his father was a Greek. Timothy was well thought of by the believers in Lystra and Iconium, so Paul wanted him to join them on their journey.
>
> Acts 16:1-2 (NLT)

It doesn't appear that the early church looked for volunteers as much as they used the personal invitation.

We recently had someone just show up for one of our training meetings. He came in, sat down and revealed, "I thought I'd sit in on your meeting." It was awkward. Kicking him out of the gathering seemed a bit extreme, and I wasn't really ready for him, but we simply proceeded with our meeting anyway. When our team members started debating whether Haddon Robinson's definition of expository preaching was accurate or if Tim Keller had a better idea, I glanced over to check in on the guest, he seemed unfazed. Then the group started discussing what tools to use for exegesis and different ways of creating tension in a talk. I again looked over at the newcomer and again he seemed okay. When we dismissed he left the building before I could debrief with him.

The next time I ran into this teaching-team meeting crasher, I was prepared with a solution. I approached him: "Hey, let me invite you to join in at the beginning the next time we start a teacher training group," I said. "It's a bit difficult to jump into the middle…" Then he jumped into the middle of my sentence. "I don't ever want to go to your group again, that is definitely NOT for me!"

The personal invitation weeds out those who would only be wasting their time. And it honors those who actually feel a call to speaking. I've had a number of folks break into tears when I merely asked them to join our group. I'm pretty sure they were happy tears by the way!

2. Make no promises

Later, Paul wrote to Timothy advising, "They must first prove themselves. Then if no one has anything against them, they can serve" (1 Timothy 3:10, CEV).

Allow time to discover a candidate's gifts before pushing him or her on stage.

Let the trainees know that agreeing to sit in on training does not guarantee that they will be preaching on Sunday. I've had to be very clear that this is an invitation to a training team first, not an invitation to preach the Easter Sunday sermon.

I'd also suggest refraining from making any promises *not* to ask them to speak as well. I've encouraged some people to join the group. "Don't worry about us asking you to speak, we won't do that…" Then we asked them to speak, and they did great, so we asked them to speak again, and they keep bringing up, "But you promised not to…"

Let's be very clear from the beginning.

3. Work through solid materials

> Meanwhile a Jew named Apollos, a native of Alexandria, came to Ephesus. He was a learned man, with a thorough knowledge of the Scriptures. He had been instructed in the way of the Lord, and he spoke with great fervor and taught about Jesus accurately, though he knew only the baptism of John. He began to speak boldly in the synagogue. When Priscilla and Aquila heard him, they invited him to their home and explained to him the way of God more adequately.
>
> Acts 18:24-26 (NIV)

Our teaching training involves ongoing study through preaching and speaking books and resources.

We start our potential speakers with Andy Stanley's *Communicating for a Change*. This is the best preaching primer I've seen. The work is readable; it captures the primary reason for teaching – changed lives; it provides a workable outline – Me, We, God, You, We – which we require each new speaker to start with if they are going to do a presentation in one of our ministries; and it hits just about every aspect of speaking.

Stanley writes, "Preaching for life change requires far less information and more application. Less explanation and more inspiration. Less first century and more twenty-first century."[36]

Many folks will push back on Stanley's one point "Big Idea." Some will fight the "Me-We-God-You-We" format. We encourage them to follow this method anyway. It gives us great insight as to whether they know how to follow and are willing to learn or change. Just about everyone who follows Stanley's approach – even reluctantly – ends up appreciating and even liking it.

Jim Kennon leads an Excel Leadership Network Preaching Cohort in the Phoenix area. He recently sent me this note: "Going over Andy Stanley's *Communicating for a Change* has (once again) disturbed my comfort zone as a communicator. A few weeks ago, I found myself just staring at the passage for three days – waiting for the aha moment to discover the one main truth. It was painful just waiting. Then on Thursday the moment came, the fog cleared, and the message basically prepared itself. Time (and agony) well spent. Thanks, Andy, and thanks, Cohort."

The next book we work through is Haddon Robinson's classic, *Biblical Preaching*. Andy Stanley borrowed the term "Big Idea" from Haddon Robinson. *Biblical Preaching* has been the top preaching book in seminaries and Bible schools for decades. Since it was written as a seminary

---

36 Andy Stanley and Lane Jones, *Communicating for a Change: Seven Keys to Irresistible Communication* (Sisters, Or.: Multnomah Publishers, 2006).

textbook it isn't the easiest book to digest. How a student responds to this gives us insight on their work ethic and ability to grapple with complicated concepts.

Robinson gives the classic definition of expository preaching: "Expository preaching is the communication of a biblical concept, derived from and transmitted through a historical, grammatical, and literary study of a passage in its context, which the Holy Spirit first applies to the personality and experience of the preacher, then through the preacher, applies to the hearers."[37]

After taking our first teaching team through these two landmark volumes, I began to look for the next obvious book to study. I was hit with a giant pile of nothing. I asked quite a few friends for recommendations, and even inquired of some seminary preaching professors on their ideas. Crickets. Seriously, no one had any ideas. Then I asked Paul Borden, he immediately suggested Eugene Lowry's *The Homiletical Plot.*

This book was originally published in 1980 and fairly difficult to find when we were looking, but it has been reissued and expanded. If Andy Stanley derived the "Big Idea" from Haddon Robinson, he borrowed, "Me-We-God-You-We" from Eugene Lowry. Lowry used the terms, "Oops! – Ugh! – Aha! – Whee! – Yeah!" which is known as the "Lowry Loop." This work suggests sermons take on more of the formula of a television drama than the old, "three-points-and-a-poem" structure. Unfortunately, Lowry doesn't heed his own advice. It isn't written in

---

37   Haddon W. Robinson, *Biblical Preaching: The Development and Delivery of Expository Messages* (Grand Rapids, MI: Baker Academic, 2001), Kindle Edition, Locations 235-237.

dramatic form, it is written like required reading in a seminary homiletics class, but it is still a must-read.

Eugene Lowry argues that even if preachers are not preaching on a biblical story, the points of the sermon should nevertheless feel like the parts of a narrative.

After working through these three I set out to find the next training book. I asked Dale Hummel for a suggestion and he recommended going through *Save The Cat! The Last Book on Screenwriting You'll Ever Need* by Blake Snyder.

As the byline indicates, this is a treatise on how to write a screenplay. It is an entertaining look at how narratives can be put together, the plot lines and B-stories and tension. There are great tips on getting away from your writing for a time and how to set up the particular pieces in a story. It was a fun study after working through two heavy tomes, and it complimented Lowry's book splendidly.

Snyder says, "Whether you're writing a comedy, a drama, or a sci-fi monster picture, a good movie has to be 'about something.' And the place to stick what your movie is about is right up front. Say it! Out loud. Right there. If you don't have a movie that's about something, you're in trouble. Strive to figure out what it is you're trying to say. Maybe you won't know until your first draft is done. But once you do know, be certain that the subject is raised right up front – page 5 is where I always put it. But make sure it's there. It's your opening bid. Declare: I can prove it. Then set out to do so."[38]

---

38 Blake Snyder, *Save the Cat!: The Last Book on Screenwriting You'll Ever Need* (Studio City, CA: Michael Wiese, 2005), Kindle Edition, 74.

The next book I would take the team through is Timothy Keller's *Preaching*. Keller has forgotten more about preaching than our team might ever learn. He cites so many preaching books I wonder why I was ever stumped about what to study next. Many of the books he alludes to are actually out of print. Where did *he* find them?

Keller reveals, "I concluded that the difference between a bad sermon and a good sermon is largely located in the preachers – in their gifts and skills and in their preparation for any particular message. However, while the difference between a bad sermon and a good sermon is mainly the responsibility of the preacher, the difference between good preaching and great preaching lies mainly in the work of the Holy Spirit in the heart of the listener as well as the preacher."[39]

We have also finished working though:

Talk Like Ted: The 9 Public-Speaking Secrets of the World's Top Minds by Carmine Gallo – a great look at how the best Ted Talk presenters master their craft. Gallo writes, "I can teach you how to tell a story. I can teach you how to design a gorgeous PowerPoint slide. I can even teach you how to use your voice and body more effectively. Effective stories, slides, and body language are important components of a persuasive presentation, yet they mean little if the speaker isn't passionate about his or her topic. The first step to inspiring others is to make sure you're inspired yourself."[40]

---

39 Timothy Keller, *Preaching: Communicating Faith in an Age of Skepticism* (New York, NY: Penguin Books, 2016), Kindle Edition.

40 Gallo, *Talk like TED*.

Dying to Preach: Embracing the Cross in the Pulpit by Steven Smith – a reminder of the tough work of preaching. Here is Smith's premise: "Preaching is not a display case for rhetorical capability; it is not a place to show how traditional or trendy we are; it is not a place to fulfill aspirations of glory. The pulpit is a place to die so that others might live."[41]

Preaching by Fred Craddock – a bit dated but worth the time. Craddock ended his book with this: "And who can conceive of any greater motivation for preaching our very best than this: there is at least one person in the sanctuary listening, one person who, because of this sermon, may have a clearer vision, a brighter hope, a deeper faith, a fuller love. That person is the preacher."[42]

Preaching for God's Glory by Allister Begg – Chapter 5 is an excellent resource for any preacher: Think Yourself Empty/Read Yourself Full/Write Yourself Clear/ Pray Yourself Hot/Be Yourself but don't Preach Yourself. I heard Albert Tate give an excellent presentation on this material – it was so good, we went through the book!

Deep & Wide by Andy Stanley – specifically chapter eleven on "Double-Barrel Preaching." Stanley outlines how to speak to engaged believers and unchurched folks with the same sermon. He claims, "The key to successfully engaging unchurched people in a weekend message has more to do with your approach and your presentation than your content."[43]

---

41 Steven W. Smith, *Dying to Preach: Embracing the Cross in the Pulpit* (Grand Rapids, MI: Kregel Publications, 2009), Kindle Edition, Locations 193-194.

42 Fred B. Craddock, *Preaching* (Nashville: Abingdon Press, 2010), Kindle Edition, 222.

43 Andy Stanley, *Deep & Wide: Creating Churches Unchurched People Love to Attend* (Grand Rapids, MI: Zondervan, 2016), Kindle Edition, 230.

The Art of the Pitch: Persuasion and Presentation Skills that Win by Peter Coughter – Coughter is an advertising pitch man. He claims "everything is a presentation," then he delivers incredible insights on presenting, speaking, and winning. Many preaching books focus on content – and this is absolutely necessary – but I like, *The Art of the Pitch* because it focuses on the presentation. Coughter brings up issues like how we can hold on to presentation distractions for years if we're not careful, and he warns against coming off as a Game Show Host: "It isn't unusual for me to encounter a presenter who is confident in his ability, knows his stuff, and has been very successful in the past. At least, in his own mind. What he doesn't realize is that what he thinks of as "polished" is actually coming off as "slick."

> The primary benefit for training time isn't so much *what* we discuss as much as it is *that* we discuss.

Audiences don't like "slick." "Slick" is a synonym for "inauthentic." And "inauthentic" really is deadly. So it's got to be stamped out."[44] This is a great book; I'd put it high on any list for training.

Preaching the Other Way, another book our team has worked through, by an author I know pretty well.

Saying It Well: The Art and Practice of Successful Speaking by Charles Swindoll – this is the book we are currently working through. Swindoll emphasizes that "...anyone can become an effective public speaker if he or she wants to work hard."[45]

---

44 Coughter, *Art of the Pitch*, Kindle Edition, 88.
45 Swindoll, *Saying It Well*, Kindle Edition, 32.

Other books we have distributed to our team include: *Saving Eutychus: How to Preach and Keep People Awake* by Gary Millar and Phil Campbell – an admirable work on keeping and holding listener's attention. "Another danger," Millar says, "stems from the fact that people place far too much emphasis on the preacher as 'performer' (or even 'personality')."[46]

We are looking at reviewing *The Laws of Communication for Preaching* by Dave Snyder. Snyder boldly claims, "I believe everyone has potential to become a world-class communicator and preacher."[47]

Other works in the queue are, *Recapturing the Voice of God* by Steven Smith; *Preaching that Moves People* by Yancey Arrington; *Homilies to Transform Hearts and Minds* by Andre Papineau; and *Biblical Sermons* by Haddon Robinson.

We continue to look for challenging materials to help us become better presenters. (I'm counting our outing to see Jerry Seinfeld do a live comedy routine as training time!)

But honestly, the primary benefit for training time isn't so much *what* we discuss as much as it is *that* we discuss.

In his work *Why Johnny Can't Preach*, David Gordon postulates that one reason Johnny can't preach is because Johnny can't read, or more specifically, doesn't read or study: "A culture that reads can consider what is significant because reading takes time, and that which is significant ordinarily takes time to apprehend. But a culture that

---

46   J. G. Millar and Phil Campbell, *Saving Eutychus: How to Preach Gods Word and Keep People Awake* (Kingsford, Australia: Matthias Media, 2013), Kindle Edition, Locations 163-164.

47   Snyder, *The Laws of Communication for Preaching*, Kindle Edition, 11.

is accustomed to commercial interruptions every six or seven minutes loses its ability to discuss significant matters because it has lost the patience necessary to consider them."[48]

Luke says, "Saul's preaching became more and more powerful..." (Acts 9:22, NLT).

We can follow in Paul's footsteps and become better at preaching while we help others become more powerful preachers too.

Rhythm and Style

A St. Charles, Illinois, newspaper ran this headline: "450 Sheep Jump to Their Deaths in Turkey." The story began, "Shepherds eating breakfast outside the town of Gevas, Turkey, were surprised to see a lone sheep jump off of a nearby cliff and fall to its death. They were stunned, however, when the rest of the nearly 1,500 sheep in the herd followed, each leaping off of the same cliff."

When it was all over, the local newspaper reported that "450 of the sheep perished in a billowy, white pile" (those that jumped from the middle and end of the herd were saved as the pile became higher and the fall more cushioned). The estimated loss to the families of Gevas tops $100,000 – an extremely significant amount of money in a country where the average person earns about $2,700 annually.

"There's nothing we can do. They're all wasted," said Nevzat Bayhan, a member of one of the twenty-six families whose sheep were grazing together in the herd.

---

48   T. David Gordon, *Why Johnny Can't Preach: The Media Have Shaped the Messengers* (Phillipsburg, NJ: P & R Pub., 2009), Kindle Edition, Locations 488-491.

Too often we blindly follow other folks who are leaping to their demise. In developing a teaching team, we are not trying to create blind followers who jump at everything we ask. And there is something we can do to prevent inauthentic imitation.

When I originally asked one of our top, current teaching team contributors if he would join the team he immediately declined. "I could never speak like you," he said. I responded, "Who wants to speak like me? A lot of the time I don't actually want to speak like me!"

My preaching style is weird. I tell a lot of jokes and use a ton of humor.

I identify with Charles Spurgeon who was once chided for using too much humor in his talks. He replied, "If only you knew how much I hold back, you would commend me. There are things in these sermons that may produce smiles, but what of them? I am not quite sure about a smile being a sin, and at any rate I think it less a crime to cause a momentary laughter than a half hour of profound slumber."

The great German preacher Helmit Thieleke remarked. "A church is in a bad way when it banishes laughter from the pulpit and leaves it to the cabaret, the night-club, and the toastmasters."

You've got to love a preacher named "Helmit." Do you think he wore one?

Anyway, storytelling is my strength. I've been accused once or twice of giving a sky-scraper sermon – one story after another.

Anyone who would try to mimic my preaching style would get confused and eventually quit. We are not trying to manufacture clones through a teaching team. Yes, we push a starting pattern and we read through the same preaching materials together. But we encourage our players to find their own style. It will take some time, experience, failure, and success to discover your rhythm and style, but keep at it and embrace how God wired you.

Judy Garland said, "Always be a first-rate version of yourself instead of a second-rate version of somebody else."

That great preacher-from-another-time Phillips Brooks affirmed, "Preaching is truth mediated through personality." Discern and embrace your own personality and allow God to use you.

Peter Coughter affirmed, "Forget about being 'professional,' and start being yourself. Your authentic self."[49]

One of the key members of our teaching team, Ben Finney, is also a high school math teacher. Ben is on a traditional schedule with summers off from teaching. A few years ago he started a tradition of watching at least one full movie series each summer break. He started with a short one, the *Back to the Future* trilogy. He worked through the entire *Star Wars* series one summer. On his latest break, Ben watched all of the *Mission:Impossible* films. Ben said he noticed that in most series, the producers try to tie them together with similar scenes or themes in each movie. For example, in the *Mission:Impossible* series, each movie contains one scene where Tom Cruise's character

> **Discern and embrace your own personality and allow God to use you.**

---

49   Coughter, *Art of the Pitch*, Kindle Edition, 12.

falls from a significant height only to stop inches from the ground. Ben says the common themes unite the films, and he found himself waiting for the falling scene in each of the *M:I* shows.

Then Finney observed, "In our teaching team, we bring our different personalities and styles, but common scenes tie the messages and series together." In each message, no matter who is speaking, we try to bring in two familiar "scenes." Ben suggests that regular congregants find themselves waiting for those scenes.

One is a clear gospel presentation using the "ABC Prayer." No matter who is speaking, we make sure to tie the message together by outlining our need to interact with the gospel by admitting we need a savior, believing Jesus died and rose gain to offer us forgiveness, and committing to follow him.

The second "scene" is what our Lead Pastor, Tim Pearring, calls "The Big Challenge." Each message, no matter who is presenting, contains a clear, measurable action step to make it easy for folks to apply the sermon and progress on their spiritual journey.

MINI-CASE-STUDY:
DISCIPLES CHURCH, FOLSOM, CALIFORNIA

Disciples' preaching team has six to eight members on it, with two to three who regularly preach in Sunday services. They meet monthly to watch each other's preaching on video, outline new series, and brainstorm long-term preaching direction.

Lead Pastor Stu Streeter says, "Our main reason for starting a Preaching Team was simply to raise up others in our congregation who had a gift but had not sharpened the skills and practice around the gift. It has also served us well in giving a place of service to those who have a passion for the direction of preaching in our church, to weigh in and help guide us directionally.

Training consists of reading books on communication together and watching each other regularly on video to evaluate sermon delivery. Disciples uses a simple evaluation sheet to help give some quantitative reflection on a sermon.

Streeter cites these advantages: "First and foremost, the congregation is getting different perspectives in a series. For example, we are currently studying The Miraculous as it appears in the Book of Acts. To have all of those insights and challenges come from *my* reading of Acts would leave the church short. Our other preacher in this series brought a tremendous depth of insight and challenge to our people that I never could have."

He says team teaching further helps to "develop the gifts and skills of communicators in our congregation. Getting training on preaching is typically reserved for the seminarian. By having a preaching team, we are able to pull back the curtain on the inner-workings of a sermon series – from raw idea, to a Sunday morning."

Streeter concludes, "We have challenged people's preferences in worship music, volume, and style for decades. Introducing a preaching team now challenges people's preferences on another level. For those bound and determined to be consumers in church, this does not go well."

THE BIG CHALLENGE:

Go back through the list of books listed in this chapter and choose one to read and discuss with your teaching team. Take turns having the members lead the discussions as another opportunity for practice in communication.

CHAPTER 12

WHO IS GIVING YOU FEEDBACK?

If you don't listen to what people say, pretty soon you will have surrounded yourself with people who have nothing to say.

—Andy Stanley

It doesn't matter how old you are or what you think you've accomplished. You don't know everything. If you let your success harden into stubbornness, you may actually know less as the years go on. You get stupider because you stop listening. Nobody can tell you anything.

—John Calipari, *Players First: Coaching from the Inside Out*

As soon as possible, experts hungrily seek feedback on how they did. Necessarily, much of that feedback is negative. This means that experts are more interested in what they did wrong - so they can fix it - than what they did right. The active processing of this feedback is as essential as its immediacy.

—Angela Duckworth, *Grit: The Power of Passion and Perseverance*

S tudents were required to wear a suit to homiletics class on the days they were scheduled to preach. Everyone knew it was my day when I showed up to Denver Seminary sporting a light blue three-piece getup. "Pearring must be preaching today," they joked.

It was my first graduate school speech and I was fighting nerves when I walked into Dr. James Means' preaching class. It was comforting to know I wasn't the only one speaking that period. My good friend, my fraternity brother who helped lead me to the Lord and fellow UCLA alumnus Rick Siemens, was also on the docket.

Dr. Means trudged into class a bit late that day. His face was more grim than normal, and he abruptly announced, "My brother-in-law dropped dead last night. Immediately after this class I'm driving to Kansas for the funeral. So, I'm in no mood..." Then he added, "Siemens called in sick, so Pearring you are up."

Shaken, I proceeded to deliver a well-prepared, lackluster, very organized, mediocre attempt at a message and then sat down. In a word, it was forgettable. What wasn't forgettable was what happened next. I was expecting that we'd be dismissed early, but instead Dr. Means rolled a television monitor and VCR to the front of the class. "Since Siemens isn't here, and we have some time, let's play Pearring's message again and I'll make comments."

No one likes to be honest with their pastor.

Means' comments were, well, mean. He ripped into this first seminary talk like someone who had just experienced a death in his family. He said, "I've seen preachers get more excited about the little boys underwear section of the Sears and Roebuck catalogue than Pearring is about this message." I remember that line, because I've never heard a preacher get excited about that kind of thing, and especially since Dr. Means used that line more than once or twice!

Immediately many of my classmates came to my defense: "It wasn't that bad Dr. Means." "You've got to admit the jokes were pretty funny."

Dr. Means wasn't convinced. He rushed out after class. My friends came up to console me, but I remember smiling. I felt pretty good about the experience.

Why? I had actually received some real feedback. I figured God had a plan for my speaking future if he allowed me to go through something like that. And even better, my friend Rick owed me *big time*.

Who gives feedback to preachers?

I once showed up an hour and forty-five minutes late for a wedding I was scheduled to officiate. Everyone – especially the betrothed couple – only had nice things to say. I deserved a scolding, but no one likes to be honest with their pastor.

Once, after what I believe is the worst sermon I have ever given (I had hives, an in-message interview went poorly, and I wasn't as prepared as I should have been), person by person shook my hand and commented, "Nice job, Pastor." Finally, I couldn't take it. "Seriously?" I asked. "That was not a good sermon." My son Tim was standing about ten feet away. He overheard the exchange and laughed, "Dad, you're right. That was terrible!"

Curt Harlow from Bayside Church in Granite Bay, California, says, "No great communication happens without an editorial process, but in most American churches the pastor doesn't receive any feedback before or after his sermon. Nothing that really matters in the world goes without the editorial process except for American sermons."

Where are we going to get honest feedback?

Here's the reality:

The longer you live the less feedback you get.

It's true, isn't it? As a kid, everyone chips in their two cents: parents, older siblings, grandparents, aunts, uncles, teachers, coaches – it is a constant barrage of, "Knock it off, stop it, that's better, way to go…"

But as we age, it is less and less culturally acceptable to give feedback to people. And when we get to be older, people just don't bother. "It's 'part-timers,' he's stuck in his ways, don't mess with Grandpa…"

The longer you do something the less feedback you get.

When you start out on a job or task, there is usually some training, but once you reach journeyman status it is no longer acceptable for someone to point out anything without their being labeled a control freak or smart aleck.

The longer you lead the less feedback you get.

The more you move up the ladder in an organization, the less anyone would ever think of pointing out something you might want to work on. "It is lonely at the top" rings true, which leads to the last secret:

The longer you succeed the less feedback you get.

Author and Harvard surgeon Atul Gawande started to realize his work had slowly stagnated. One afternoon, he thought he would sneak out for a game of tennis but couldn't find a partner. Finally, he went to a local tennis club but was informed he could practice there only if he paid for a lesson and hit with the club pro.

Gawande writes what happened next:

> He was in his early twenties, a recent graduate who'd played on his college team. We hit back and forth for a while. He went easy on me at first, and then started running me around. I served a few points, and the tennis coach in him came out. "You know," he said, "you could get more power from your serve." I was dubious. My serve had always been the best part of my game. But I listened. He had me pay attention to my feet as I served, and I gradually recognized that my legs weren't really underneath me when I swung my racquet up into the air. My right leg dragged a few inches behind my body... With a few minutes of tinkering, he'd added at least ten miles an hour to my serve."[50]

Not long afterward, Gawande was watching tennis star Rafael Nadal playing a tournament match on TV.

> "The camera flashed to his coach, and the obvious struck me: even Rafael Nadal has a coach. Nearly every elite tennis player in the world does... But doctors don't. I'd paid to have a kid just out of college look at my serve. So why did I find it

---

50 Atul Gawande, "Personal Best," *New Yorker Magazine*, October 3, 2011.

inconceivable to pay someone to come into my operating room and coach me on my surgical technique?"[51]

In his book *Saving Eutychus*, Gary Millar discloses, "Over the years I've become increasingly aware that I need people in my life (in addition to my wife) who aren't afraid to say, 'Gary, that was really poor' or, 'Brother, I'm sorry to tell you that you really missed the point.' But those kinds of relationships don't come easily. We need to develop relationships with a few people whom we can trust – people who not only share our theological vision and our basic commitments about preaching, but who are also skilled at highlighting where we are prone to going wrong, and who are not afraid to say so in a loving, godly way. I suspect that a minority of preachers have these kinds of relationships."[52]

"Doctor!" said the woman as she loudly bounced into the room, "I want you to tell me very frankly what's wrong with me." He surveyed her from head to foot. "Madam," he said at length, "I've just three things to tell you. First, you are fat. You need to drop at least thirty pounds. Second, lose the makeup. You should use about half as much rouge and lipstick. And third, I'm an engineer – the doctor's office is on the next floor."

> A huge piece to developing a teaching team is creating a culture of feedback.

---

51   Ibid.
52   Millar and Campbell, *Saving Eutychus*, Kindle Edition, Locations 1403-1405.

In his book, *What to Ask the Person in the Mirror*, Robert Kaplan writes:

> When I first ask a subordinate for constructive feedback, they tend to begin by telling me that I'm doing "very well" on all fronts. When I follow up and ask, "Well, what should I be doing differently?" they respond, "Nothing that I can think of." If I challenge them by saying, "Hey – there must be something!" still they tend to say, "No, really; nothing comes to mind." I then ask them to sit back and think a little more. "We have plenty of time," I say.
>
> An awkward silence tends to ensue. Beads of sweat start appearing on their forehead. They are probably thinking, "Oh, my lord, this guy is really serious – what the heck am I supposed to say now?" At that point, in some cases, they look like they're about to speak, and then stop themselves.
>
> I then usually have to ask, "What were you about to say? Please go on and say it!" At this moment, they typically throw out something that they've been thinking but have been afraid to say. That "something" is often devastating – because it is a fundamental criticism, because I know it's accurate, and because I realize that many people in the organization probably have the same observation. Ouch!
>
> If you have ever gone through this process yourself, you know that you need to maintain your

composure, sincerely thank that person for their feedback, and then call a close friend or loved one to ask whether this criticism sounds accurate. Most likely, they will pause and say, "Well, yes, that does sound like you." OK, so you now have an agenda item to work on. You need to take steps to address this weakness – which you almost certainly can do if you are open to improving yourself.

The good news is that in my experience, I find that ninety percent of the battle is getting the feedback. Once you realize that you have a specific weakness, you can almost certainly find ways to address it and improve."[53]

A huge piece to developing a teaching team is creating a culture of feedback. How can we give and receive feedback?

1. Ask for feedback

The doorbell rang, and the lady of the house discovered a workman, complete with tool chest, on the front porch. "Madam," he announced, "I'm the piano tuner." The lady exclaimed, "Why? I didn't send for a piano tuner." The man replied, "I know you didn't, but your neighbors did."

When we first started the teaching team approach, I struggled with how I could help the other speakers. How

---

53 Robert Steven. Kaplan, *What to Ask the Person in the Mirror: Critical Questions for Becoming a More Effective Leader and Reaching Your Potential* (Boston, MA: Harvard Business Review Press, 2011), Kindle Edition, 99-100.

can I communicate some areas for them to work on without coming off as arrogant or harsh?

I had an idea, what if I asked them for feedback on my messages? If I was open to hearing their input, perhaps they would be open to hearing mine. The strategy worked amazingly.

Improving speakers seek feedback.

In *The Laws of Communication for Preaching*, Dave Snyder advises, "Who wants to go back and listen to themselves speak? It's a horrible experience. It doesn't matter how great a speaker you are or if you are a seasoned, sought after communicator, you probably hate hearing yourself speak. The only thing worse than that is watching yourself on video. But that is exactly what great communicators do."[54]

We must nurture an environment where the goal is improvement in an uplifting atmosphere.

Andy Stanley shares, "You will never figure out what works and what doesn't listening to the casual comments of your constituents. And your spouse won't be much help either. If you want to improve, you are going to have to listen to yourself and ask for constructive criticism. Neither are any fun. I would much rather listen to your CD than mine."[55]

My son Scott records and reviews all of his presentations. He says, "Listening to recordings of yourself is the most painful – and most valuable – coaching you can do."

---

54 Snyder, *The Laws of Communication for Preaching*, Kindle Edition, 154.
55 Stanley and Jones, *Communicating for a Change*, 180.

Author Derek Doepker suggests these questions for obtaining helpful responses to your efforts:

> The key to improving your work comes from quality feedback. Both 'your book sucks' and 'your book is the best thing ever' lack any real constructive insight. Neither blanket praise nor condemnation will help you improve your books, so you must learn how to dig more out from your readers. The way to do this is with high quality questions designed to get people to open up and share more about what is working and not working with your books. Some quality questions include:
>
> - What did you enjoy most about this book?
>
> - Was there anything in particular you found most helpful?
>
> - What was your favorite part and why?
>
> - What could make this even better?
>
> If you're looking for constructive feedback on how to improve your book (and you should), a great question to ask is, "How can I make this even better?"[56]

---

56   Derek Doepker, *Why Authors Fail: 17 Mistakes Self-Publishing Authors Make That Sabotage Their Success (And How To Fix Them)* (Amazon Publishing Services, 2014).

2. Advance a culture of uplifting feedback.

David Nelms says, "There is no such thing as constructive criticism. All criticism is, by nature, critical. We need to focus on feedback, not criticism."

Criticism is rampant. It's a growing, money-making industry in our culture.

> Some, however, made fun of them and said, "They have had too much wine."
>
> Acts 1:13 (NIV)

Criticism can lead to a critical spirit which seeks, often unknowingly, to tear down, condemn, and destroy.

Feedback is defined as: "Information about reactions to a product, a person's performance of a task, etc., used as a basis for improvement."

We must nurture an environment where the goal is improvement in an uplifting atmosphere.

When we hear one of our team members present during a training time, we always start with what went well. We major on the positives. Then we talk about what could be improved, and then we end with another positive note.

3. Avoid negative people.

Edgar Watson Howe advised, "Don't abuse your friends and expect them to consider it criticism."

Carey Nieuwhof added, "Don't let the people who have only sat on the sidelines tell you how to play the game."

Paul outlines some specific type of feedback in his first letter to Timothy:

You should know this, Timothy, that in the last days there will be very difficult times. For people will love only themselves and their money. They will be boastful and proud, scoffing at God, disobedient to their parents, and ungrateful. They will consider nothing sacred. They will be unloving and unforgiving; they will slander others and have no self-control. They will be cruel and hate what is good. They will betray their friends, be reckless, be puffed up with pride, and love pleasure rather than God. They will act religious, but they will reject the power that could make them godly. Stay away from people like that!

> **Don't allow consistently negative people on your team or into your head.**

1 Timothy 3:1-5 (NLT)

Paul tells us to stay away from selfish manipulators. This is a biblical theme:

A false witness will perish, and whoever listens to him will be destroyed forever.

Proverbs 21:28 (NIV)

Don't listen to everything people say...

Ecclesiastes 7:21 (NCV)

Only simpletons believe everything they're told! The prudent carefully consider their steps.

Proverbs 14:15 (NLT)

Negative Nellies, Debbie Downers, and Wally Whiners don't last long on our team. We try not to invite them, and we try to make it so positive they don't like hanging around. Seth Godin suggested:

> You won't benefit from anonymous criticism. I recently heard from a speaker who was able to quote, verbatim, truly nasty comments people had posted about her talk. And yet, I've never once met an author who said, "Well, my writing wasn't resonating, but then I read all the bad reviews on Amazon, took their criticism to heart, and now I'm doing great..."
>
> There are plenty of ways to get useful and constructive feedback. It starts with looking someone in the eye, with having a direct one-on-one conversation or email correspondence with a customer who cares. Forms, surveys, mass emails, tweets – none of this is going to do anything but depress you, confuse you (hey, half the audience wants one thing, the other half wants the opposite!) or paralyze you.
>
> I'm arguing that it's a positive habit to deliberately insulate yourself from this feedback. Don't ask for it and don't look for it. Yes, change what you make to enhance delight. No, don't punish yourself by listening to the mob.

Don't allow consistently negative people on your team or into your head.

Top Ten Feedback Lines from Golf Caddies:

10. **Golfer:** "Well Caddy, how do you like my game?"

    Caddy: *"Very good, Sir! But personally, I prefer Golf."*

9. **Golfer:** "Well, I have never played this badly before!"

    Caddy: *"I didn't realize you had played before, Sir."*

8. **Golfer:** "I'd move heaven and earth to be able to break 100 on this course."

    Caddy: *"Try heaven," advised the caddy. "You've already moved most of the earth."*

7. **Golfer:** "Caddy, do you think my game is improving?

    Caddy: *"Oh yes, sir! You miss the ball much closer than you used to."*

6. **Golfer:** "Caddy, do you think it is a sin to play golf on Sunday?"

    Caddy: *"The way you play, sir, it's a crime any day of the week!"*

5. **Golfer:** "That can't be my ball. It looks far too old."

    Caddy: *"It's been a long time since we started, sir."*

4. **Golfer:** "Do you think I can get there with a 5-iron?"

    Caddy: *"Eventually."*

3. **Golfer:** "I've played so poorly all day; I think I'm going to go drown myself in that lake."

    Caddy: *"I doubt you could keep your head down that long."*

2. **Golfer:** "This is the worst course I've ever played on."

    Caddy: *"But this isn't the golf course... We left that an hour ago, sir."*

1. **Golfer:** "You've got to be the worst caddy in the world."

    Caddy: *"I don't think so sir... That would be too much of a coincidence."*

Marshall Goldsmith writes, "Successful people only have two problems dealing with negative feedback. However, they are big problems: (a) they don't want to hear it from us and (b) we don't want to give it to them. It's not hard to see why people don't want to hear negative feedback. Successful people are incredibly delusional about their achievements. Over ninety-five percent of the members in most successful groups believe that they perform in the top half of their group. While this is statistically ridiculous, it is psychologically real. Giving people negative feedback means "proving" they are wrong. Proving to successful people that they are wrong works just about as well as making them change. Not gonna happen."[57]

4. Acquire input from godly leaders.

I intentionally use the word "acquire" because it costs to get feedback. It may cost money, it should cost time, and there will be an emotional price to pay.

> But you, Timothy, certainly know what I teach, and how I live, and what my purpose in life is. You know my faith, my patience, my love, and my endurance.
>
> 1 Timothy 3:10 (NLT)

Paul tells Timothy to stay away from the wrong kind of feedback and stay tuned to the right kind of feedback.

Why was Cinderella not good at public speaking? She had a pumpkin for a coach.

The student pilot and flight instructor were the only ones on board the small plane when it hit the runway and bounced repeatedly until it came to a stop. The instructor turned to the student and said, "That was a very bad

---

57 Marshall Goldsmith and Mark Reiter, *What Got You Here Won't Get You There: How Successful People Become Even More Successful* (New York: Hachette Books, 2014), Kindle Edition, 111.

landing you just made." "Me?" replied the student. "I thought you were landing!"

Marshall Goldsmith discovered that most people over-rate themselves when asked to compare themselves with their peers: "Successful people consistently compare themselves favorably to their peers. If you ask successful professionals to rate themselves against their peers, eighty to eighty-five percent of them will rate themselves in the top twenty percent of their peer group – and seventy percent will rate themselves in the top ten percent. This number goes even higher among professionals with higher perceived social status, such as physicians, pilots, and investment bankers, ninety percent of whom place themselves in the top ten percent."[58]

> **To become more effective, we need to get feedback – and listen to it!**

I suspect preachers probably rate themselves too highly as well.

Here's an excerpt from James Merritt's article, "Ministry Meltdown." He was having trouble in life and he entered into a year-long commitment with a leadership coach named Fred.

> Fred has seen hundreds of CEO types, and he says the success rate is around 40 percent. The other 60 percent continue to stumble and often end up losing their jobs and families. He said the difference is humility. Those who turn the corner and take their

---

58 Goldsmith and Reiter, *What Got You Here Won't Get You There*, Kindle Edition, 19-20.

leadership and lives to a new level are those who are humble enough to receive feedback and take it seriously.

To become more effective, we need to get feedback – and listen to it! A while back, Lori and I flew to Seattle to meet with our future son-in-law, Waison, and my daughter, Tricia. The meeting had one purpose – Waison was going to ask for our daughter's hand in marriage. My youngest son, Jake, called me up with some advice. "Dad, when Waison asks you if he can marry Tricia, resist the urge to respond with a joke."

That is some of the best advice I have ever received. And when Waison asked, I didn't jest, I just cried uncontrollably. Tricia and Waison are now married, and I'm sensing Jake is feeling more free to offer feedback.

5. Access the manual

Todd Stocker declared, "A speaker should approach his preparation not by what he wants to say, but by what he wants to learn."

Paul ends his session on feedback with this:

> All Scripture is inspired by God and is useful to teach us what is true and to make us realize what is wrong in our lives. It corrects us when we are wrong and teaches us to do what is right. God uses it to prepare and equip his people to do every good work.
>
> 2 Timothy 3:16-17 (NLT)

Paul reminds us that the best feedback comes from God and His Word. Are we letting God give us input?

> Be strong and very courageous. Be careful to obey all the law my servant Moses gave you; do not turn from it to the right or to the left, that you may be successful wherever you go. Keep this Book of the Law always on your lips; meditate on it day and night, so that you may be careful to do everything written in it. Then you will be prosperous and successful.
>
> Joshua 1:7-8 (NIV)

> This is why I remind you to fan into flames the spiritual gift God gave you...
>
> 2 Timothy 1:6 (NIV)

> Strategic planning is the key to warfare; to win, you need a lot of good counsel.
>
> Proverbs 24:6 (TMV)

Peter Scazzero admitted, "After preaching for twenty-five years here's one surprising lesson: God wants to transform my soul through the sermon prep process. Notice I did not say God wants to transform me through my sermon or through his Word. I believe that happens too, but I often see preachers underestimating what God can do as we prepare the sermon." Scazzero calls this process "The Life Cycle of the Sermon." It's a cycle that follows a familiar pattern: birth (you get the sermon idea), death (you struggle to put the sermon together), burial (it gets even worse), resurrection (you preach it), ascension (you leave your sermon in God's hands).

6. Always collect

The Apostle Paul began one of his sermons this way: "Men of Athens, I notice that you are very religious in every way, for as I was walking along I saw your many shrines. And one of your altars had this inscription on it: 'To an Unknown God.' This God, whom you worship without knowing, is the one I'm telling you about" (Acts 17:22-23, NLT).

Perhaps Paul came up with that introduction off the top of his head, but considering his studiousness, I suspect he worked at his message illustrations.

Solomon said, "Go to the ant, you sluggard; consider its ways and be wise! It has no commander, no overseer or ruler, yet it stores its provisions in summer and gathers its food at harvest" (Proverbs 6:6-8, NIV).

Haddon Robinson made me collect illustrations. My grades depended on it. So I stopped collecting baseball cards and started collecting jokes, stories, cartoons, book excerpts, top ten lists, sermon ideas, and series starters.

I began over thirty-five years ago by purchasing an accordion file folder. The tabs were listed from A to Z and I'd slip potential illustrations into the various pockets. One of my colleagues, Dave Timmerman asked me, "What are you going to do when the folder is full?" I remember thinking, "That will never happen…"

The folder filled up, so I moved to a single-drawer filing cabinet; then a two-drawer; then four-drawer; then multiple four-drawer cabinets. I added a three-by-five index card box; then a longer one; soon my eyes became dim, I couldn't read those very well, so I went to a four-by-six index-card box.

My office started filling up. The illustrations were piling up and growing in on me. The whole process became more cumbersome than necessary, so I went to electronic collecting. I'd have a file for each month. Now I use Evernote.com. The discipline is to collect daily. Rarely does a day go by when I don't put some story, quip, quote, or joke into my files.

> **A secret to a good sermon is the meeting before the meeting.**

We've worked that into our training times. The team members are to come prepared to share at least one illustration with the group.

The Meeting Before the Meeting

In *Leadership Gold: Lessons I've Learned from a Lifetime of Leading*, John Maxwell says that the secret to a good meeting is the meeting before the meeting. Then he suggests, "If you can't have the meeting before the meeting, don't have the meeting."[59]

A secret to a good sermon is the meeting before the meeting.

Our teaching team often meets on Saturdays where one of our agenda items is to have the speaker for Sunday walk through the upcoming message. Our teaching team also always meets early on Sundays where the speaker does a

---

59   John C. Maxwell, *Leadership Gold: Lessons I've Learned from a Lifetime of Leading* (Nashville: Thomas Nelson, 2008).

quick run-through of what he or she will present in the service.

We have found that the best feedback comes before the presentation.

Maxwell adds, "The meeting before the meeting helps you avoid being blindsided: Good leaders are usually pretty good at knowing what's going on. They have strong leadership intuition. They are connected to their people. They usually have a good handle on the intangibles, such as morale, momentum, culture, etc. But even the best leaders can miss something. Sometimes during the meeting before the meeting, the person they're talking to gives them information or insight that will help them avoid making a big leadership mistake."[60]

We also have a meeting in between the meetings. In between services, the teaching team goes off to the side for in-game adjustments. We ask the speaker to start this meeting by telling us how they thought they did? In fact, "How do you think it went?" is usually the first question.

Whoever is speaking that day then asks, "Okay, let me have it. What do I need to change? Did that video work? How about that personal illustration, was it too long? Help me out." That simple meeting has improved all of us on the team by at least a full letter grade!

Recently I gave what I considered one of my best messages. Seriously, I thought it was a winner. When I asked my team members for input, one said, "Why can't my

---

60   Ibid.

messages come together like that?" Another said, "Perfect!" Then another (my son) started in, "First, you need to start by telling people you are sick…" I realized that I hadn't even considered how my cold was affecting my delivery. I really needed that input.

Since we are very limited on time (typically we have five to seven minutes) each person will make suggestions on how to improve the talk. If the speaker is especially discouraged, we take time to build them up, but mostly there isn't much time for anything but adjustments. Since our team members understand this, and we've worked hard to instill an attitude of encouragement, we can make quick suggestions without necessarily couching them in flowery language. Guest speakers have told us they felt the meeting-in-between the meetings can be brutal. We try to slip in a few kudos, "Good job!" or "That illustration was perfect," but mostly it's about changes that need to be made heading into the next service.

The Missing Two Words

Troy McMahon says the key to leadership development can be found in the missing two words.

When we think of delegation, training, and reproduction, we typically go through the following stages:

> I do it, you watch.
> I do it, you help.
> You do it, I help.
> You do it, I watch.
> You do it, someone else watches.

This is the classic leadership development timeline. But something is missing – the two words.

I do it, you watch, we discuss.
I do it, you help, we discuss.
You do it, I help, we discuss.
You do it, I watch, we discuss.
You do it, someone else watches, we discuss.

The meeting after the meeting might be just as important as any part of the meeting!

In his book *What Got You Here Won't Get You There*, Marshall Goldsmith calls these feedback meeting, feedforwarding: "I teach them the miracle of feedforward, which is my 'special sauce' methodology for eliciting advice from people on what they can do to get better in the future."

Howard Hendricks says, "Experience doesn't make you better. Only evaluated experience makes you better."

David Gordon rants, "So why don't churches routinely conduct annual reviews of their ministers? Because ministers don't want to be told that their preaching is disorganized, hard to follow, irrelevant, and poorly reasoned; and because churches don't want to insult their ministers or hurt their feelings (and churches often know that the review would have some negative aspects). Therefore, I suggest that the very absence of annual reviews stands as glaring proof that preaching is so bad today that no one – neither the preacher nor the hearer – can tolerate

> **The meeting after the meeting might be just as important as any part of the meeting!**

the thought of how painful it would be to provide an honest assessment."[61]

Let's utilize the two words: "Let's discuss."

MINI-CASE STUDY:
CONNECT CHURCH, MESA, ARIZONA

Lead Pastor David Harris says, "People learn from a host of differing personalities and styles. Not everyone will connect with my style and approach. Multiple voices/styles give us a better chance of connecting with our entire body, both now and in the future. Additionally, it gives me the opportunity to invest more of myself into other leadership and ministry areas."

The team collaboratively plans the preaching calendar for an entire year. Then they identify the specific topics or scriptures based on personal expertise and assign the preaching dates according to the calendar.

Harris admits, "In the staff hiring process, one of the elements I am looking for in a staff person (children, students, groups, etc.) is the speaking potential, though they are not necessarily told this up front. Another filter is how different are they from me stylistically.

"Team teaching allows our church to hear and learn from multiple voices and styles. It shows a willing humility on the part of the senior pastor. As a senior pastor, it also frees me up to spend larger chunks of time on leadership

---

61 Gordon, *Why Johnny Can't Preach*, Kindle Edition, Locations 291-296.

initiatives and matters, as well as granting me mental rest, which refreshes my creativity."

Connect Church strives to have at least three speakers on the team. Harris has developed a Public Speaking and Communication Dynamics course that he teaches in colleges, seminaries and conferences. Even those who do announcements go through the course. The team also sits with the speaker of the week, along with the entire teaching team, and they go over the video from Sunday ("Much like an NFL coaching staff might do.")

Harris says the downsides of team teaching are minimal, but include the leader not getting to preach as frequently as he or she might like; the risk of a lesser qualified speaker not doing well and people responding negatively; and, depending on the age/generation of the church, some of the "old-timers" feeling the senior pastor isn't doing his job.

THE BIG CHALLENGE:

Establish a time before each service begins for members of the teaching team to meet with the speaker that day to provide some last-minute feedback and encouragement. Don't forget to pray!

CHAPTER 13

FIGHT THROUGH FAILURE

You win some, lose some, and wreck some.

—Dale Earnhardt

The pain is part of the path.

—Brad Stevens, Boston Celtics coach

If I wasn't making mistakes, I wasn't making decisions.

—Robert Wood "General" Johnson II of Johnson & Johnson

have made my share of preaching mistakes. The very first sermon I ever gave, my then-fiancé, Lori, was in the audience and I asked her how it went. She said, "It was hard to tell because the guy behind me was snoring so loud." I wish I made that up!

I once began a message by saying, "Let's close in prayer." Perhaps my subconscious knew it was a bad message. One time I was so filled with cold medication I spaced out right in the middle of my talk.

Returning from vacation one time, I called the guest speaker I had scheduled to preach for me while I was away and asked how it went.

"Haven't you heard?" he responded.

"You are the first person I've contacted," I admitted.

"Well," he said, "It was short." He explained that as soon as he stepped up to preach he had a sudden urge to vomit and he threw up right on stage – twice. Church was let out early that day.

Another guest speaker I scheduled actually fell off the stage into the piano when he was making a point.

In his book *The Art of the Pitch*, Peter Coughter says, "In public opinion polls, when asked their greatest personal fear, Americans rank public speaking as number one. Number one – ahead of death. That's pretty amazing when you first think about it, but after a while it begins to make some sense. We're all afraid of embarrassing ourselves in front of a group of people, of making such fools of ourselves that we'll never live it down. Of being naked while the whole world is wearing clothes. Whereas we can go off quietly by ourselves and die. No one even has to be around. It's simple, it's just over. But speaking in front of a group of other human beings – now that's truly terrifying. I really don't mean to be flip about a subject as weighty as dying, but that's what the research indicates. I guess that may be where the term 'a fate worse than death' originated."[62]

We all make mistakes when it comes to preaching. But perhaps no mistake was as egregious as the one the Apostle Paul made:

> On the first day of the week, we gathered with the local believers to share in the Lord's Supper. Paul was preaching to them, and since he was leaving the next day, he kept talking until midnight. The upstairs room where we met was lighted with many

---

62   Coughter, *Art of the Pitch*, Kindle Edition, 77-78.

flickering lamps. As Paul spoke on and on, a young man named Eutychus, sitting on the windowsill, became very drowsy. Finally, he fell sound asleep and dropped three stories to his death below.

Acts 20:7-9 (NLT)

Paul preached so long a young man ended up falling asleep and falling to his death.

I've made a lot of mistakes preaching, but I haven't caused anyone to fall asleep and fall to his death.

Gary Millar admits in his book, *Saving Eutychus*: "But the humbling point we want to make is that what took Paul many hours of speaking to achieve – near-fatal napping – takes most of us only a few minutes speaking to a well-rested and caffeinated crowd on a Sunday."[63]

The story of Eutychus's death could have been so debilitating for Paul. He could have quit, he could have concluded that he didn't have a preaching gift. He could have turned against preaching. But he didn't do any of those things.

Paul went down, bent over him, and took him into his arms. "Don't worry," he said, "he's alive!" Then they all went back upstairs, shared in the Lord's Supper, and ate together. Paul continued talking to them until dawn, and then he left. Meanwhile, the young man was taken home alive and well, and everyone was greatly relieved.

Acts 20:10-12 (NLT)

---

63   Millar and Campbell, *Saving Eutychus*, Kindle Edition, 101-102.

Paul fought through failure – as a preacher and a leader.

> John was with them as their helper.
>
> Acts 13:5 (NLT)

> Paul and his companions sailed to Perga… where John left them to return to Jerusalem.
>
> Acts 13:13 (NLT)

Leadership development is difficult. John, also knows as Mark, only lasted eight verses with Barnabas and Paul. I'm sure they were aggravated by his desertion.

Later Paul declares:

> Everyone abandoned me…
>
> 2 Timothy 4:16 (NLT)

I believe in team teaching. Our church and our cohorts have seen great success with it. But don't think for a second that we haven't had our share of failures.

Not everyone who starts on our teaching training process finishes. Some quit because it actually involves work. Some realize teaching isn't in their gift-mix. We've had enough candidates with some sort of emotional attachment disorder that when we moved in closer, they moved on immediately.

If you want a clean, carefree life, preaching isn't for you.

Not everyone on our teaching team succeeds. We have seen some teachers come and go. One person was nice enough and gifted enough, but he simply could not make any "in-game adjustments," or really, he simply would not make *any* adjustments. We would provide feedback and he would nod and agree and verbalize he'd change, but he never did. His was an emotional firing. He's not with our church anymore.

Solomon suggested that working with people won't be easy:

> Without oxen a stable stays clean, but you need a strong ox for a large harvest.
>
> Proverbs 14:4 (NLT)

Your stable won't remain clean if you keep any oxen in it. If you want a clean, carefree life, preaching isn't for you. Neither is working with a team. But if you want to make an impact, expect the oxen to mess up some. And note that sometimes oxen mess looks a lot like teaching team mess!

Not everyone on our teaching team hits a home run every time. I admit there have been a couple of times when I sat listening to someone on our team speak, and I thought, "This isn't right. Our teaching is supposed to be better than this." Sometimes it appears that we have forgotten everything we have learned.

Margaret Thatcher expressed, "You may have to fight a battle more than once to win it."

How can we look beyond the failures?

First, *appreciate the value of failing.* We overestimate the event and underestimate the process.

I suspect that Paul's long-winded message in Troas might have been his best sermon ever. He had someone die and be brought back to life all in the middle of his talk. That's pretty memorable.

Michael Jordan says that you can't really win until you've lost.

A circus performer once admitted, "Once you know that the net below will catch you, you stop worrying about falling. You actually learn to fall successfully. What that means is you can concentrate on catching the trapeze swinging toward you, and not on falling, because repeated falls in the past have convinced you that the net is strong and reliable when you do fall...The result of falling and being caught by the net is a mysterious confidence and daring on the trapeze. You fall less. Each fall makes you able to risk more."

> God has ordained that our preaching become deeper and more winsome as we are broken, humbled, and made low and desperately dependent on grace by the trials of our lives.
>
> —John Piper

What I've told myself is that I have to enjoy the anxiety. Enjoy dealing with losses. Enjoy coping with bitter disappointment, because there are millions of people who would like to be where I am, to feel what I'm feeling – even on my worst day – and they'd gladly trade places with me. So whatever's going on, however bad it feels, appreciate the fact that it's part of sports. Know that you're going to feel it, or don't do sports.

    —John Calapari, basketball coach, *Players First*

Jason Leister wrote, "The journey is far more productive if you learn to develop gratitude for the process. Which is more gratifying? To watch a child walking or to watch a child learning to walk? My choice is the latter. You get to see GROWTH happen before your eyes. The endpoints mean far less than the journey happening in real time."[64]

Second, *don't take failure personally.*

Did you hear about the sensitive burglar? He always took everything personally.

"I hope you didn't take it personally, Pastor," an embarrassed woman said after a church service, "when my husband walked out during your sermon."

"I did find it rather disconcerting," the preacher replied.

"It's not a reflection on you, sir," insisted the churchgoer. "Ralph has been walking in his sleep ever since he was a child."

A man is playing the piano softly one night in a downtown bar. In walks an elephant who goes over to the pianist, and suddenly starts to cry. "There, there", says the pianist "Do you recognize the song?" "No, no," says the elephant "I recognize the keys."

Larry Anderson, former Major League baseball pitcher, said, "If at first you don't succeed, failure may be your thing."

---

64   Jason Leister, *The Incomparable Expert* (blog), http://www.incomparableexpert.org/.

It would be natural for me, or for our team, to personalize every failure and every mistake. I could get down on myself every time one of our twenty-something guys failed to show up for a teaching team meeting.

Look what happened to the Apostle Paul when he was preaching in Lystra:

> Then some Jews arrived from Antioch and Iconium and won the crowds to their side. They stoned Paul and dragged him out of town, thinking he was dead.
>
> Acts 14:19 (NLT)

Here we see another preaching failure in Paul's life. The crowd threw rocks at Paul until they thought he was dead.

> But as the believers gathered around him, he got up and went back into the town.
>
> Acts 14:19-20 (NLT)

John Hagee states, "Paul never developed a negative attitude. He picked his bloody body up out of the dirt and went back into the city where he had almost been stoned to death, and he said, 'Hey, about that sermon I didn't finish preaching – here it is!'"

H. Stanley Judd advised, "Don't waste energy trying to cover up failure. Learn from your failures and go on to the next challenge. It's okay to fail. If you're not failing, you're not growing."

Scott Alexander in *Rhinoceros Success* reminds us, "Luckily for you, you've got that two-inch thick rhinoceros skin. Your skin is so thick you hardly feel the shots. Yes, you are a rhinoceros and you can take a lot of adversity. You almost enjoy taking the punches because you know that it is toughening you up. The more successful a rhino you become, the bigger the torpedoes are shot at you. That's alright, you are a thick-skinned, mad, charging rhinoceros, and the torpedoes will run out before you go back to being a lazy old cow in the pasture. Keep charging!"

A successful man is one who can lay a firm foundation with bricks others have thrown at him.

Third, *make failure into a lesson.*

A successful man is one who can lay a firm foundation with bricks others have thrown at him.

> I was walking down Fifth Avenue today and I found a wallet, and I was gonna keep it, rather than return it, but I thought: well, if I lost a hundred and fifty dollars, how would I feel? And I realized I would want to be taught a lesson.
>
> —Emo Philips

> Fail fast. Don't be afraid to try things. Don't be afraid to experiment. Fail fast and we'll correct. That's how we can truly find out who we are as individuals, and as a team.
>
> —John Calipari, *Players First: Coaching from the Inside Out*

We had a six-to-eight-week stretch where our church's projector wouldn't work properly. After the first week we replaced the projector, it still messed up. We replaced it again, it still acted up. We replaced all the wiring, and the computers that were powering it, and it would not cooperate. After getting totally frustrated with the entire episode, the teaching team realized this was at least an opportunity to work on presenting without projection slides. As soon as we embraced the lesson, the projector started working again.

Failing is part of the process. It can actually lead to good things.

And fourth, *put failure in perspective.*

I think of the minister who was approached after the service by a lady who said, "Pastor that was a really long, long sermon." The pastor's wife stepped in and said, "Actually, I timed that sermon, and it was not very long at all." The pastor felt better until his wife concluded, "It only seemed really, really long."

A little girl became restless as the preacher's sermon dragged on and on. Finally, she leaned over to her mother and whispered, "Mommy, if we give him the money now, will he let us go?"

Allan Cox observed, "Achievers exhibit an attitude of expectancy. This shows itself most forcefully in the way they minimize their losses. They do not grieve over failure of what might have been. Rather, the achiever looks around the corner in anticipation of the good things that await him. All he has to do, he believes, is show the determination to get there. He rejects the notion of 'can't'. As a result, he is able to open more doors than others, strike better deals and attract more energetic and resourceful people to work with him. He sets higher standards and gets others to help him meet them. He wins confidence and nurtures vitality in others. He expects to succeed...Living the expectant life is simply an act of good judgment."[65]

Failing is part of the process. It can actually lead to good things.

> I tried to make money as a kid. I had a lemonade stand for about six weeks. I made no money. I had to burn it down and collect insurance.
>
> —Brian Kiley

Fifth, *don't let failure stop you.*

Napoleon Hill, a man who devoted his life to studying successful people, concluded, "I have had the privilege of analyzing (great people) year by year, over a long period of years, and therefore the opportunity to study them at close range. So I speak from actual knowledge when I say that I found no quality save persistence that even remotely suggested the major source of their stupendous achievements."

Paul lost a teammate in John Mark. He was hit with rocks and left for dead. He even caused someone to die through his long-windedness. But he kept going.

> Each Sabbath found Paul at the synagogue, trying to convince the Jews and Greeks alike. And after

---

65   Allan Cox, *The Making of the Achiever* (Nightingale Conant, 1991).

Silas and Timothy came down from Macedonia, Paul spent all his time preaching the word. He testified to the Jews that Jesus was the Messiah. But when they opposed and insulted him, Paul shook the dust from his clothes and said, "Your blood is upon your own heads – I am innocent. From now on I will go preach to the Gentiles."

Acts 18:4-6 (NLT)

Paul failed time and time again. But he simply shook off the ill-effects and kept preaching and leading.

MINI-CASE-STUDY:
CENTRAL VALLEY COMMUNITY CHURCH, HARTFORD, SOUTH DAKOTA

Lead Pastor Chris Gorman always had at least two pastoral apprentices on staff, then later hired a full-time associate. At one point the church had three staff members and two lay elders preaching. The lead pastor usually spoke just over half the time and the staff people spoke the other half. The lay elders spoke once or twice a year.

Gorman lists these philosophical reasons behind the team approach:

1. It's good for the church to hear multiple voices.
2. It keeps things fresh. Each teacher came with a unique perspective, experience, and style.
3. It helps keep people from becoming so dependent on the lead pastor to be all in all.

4. Preparing together helps deal with blind spots and keep teachers from always gravitating to theological hobby horses.
5. It models community to the congregation. If we want people to be in community then it needs to be modeled at every level of the church, including sermon preparation.

"This is more of my personal style, but we went so far as to create an office space without walls. All our desks were in one room and we had another room to go to if we needed privacy," says Gorman. "Most weeks, whoever was teaching would do much of the exegetical work on Monday. Then on Wednesday morning the teacher would walk the team through the text, noting key points, possible outline, theological conundrums, and then we would talk out possible application. On Friday we would talk through the service in general and a part of that was to talk through the sermon and give any feedback. If it was a student who was learning they would actually teach the lesson to the staff and we would give feedback. The week was also littered with lots of unplanned conversations due to the close proximity of our offices and desks."

Central Valley had a clear training system: "Part of it is our elder training and then for those who were going to be teachers we added preaching training to it. All of our elders and pastoral apprentices had to spend a year in intensive discipleship. This included reading *The Trellis and the Vine*, Wayne Grudem's *Systematic Theology*, and Michael Lawrence's *Biblical Theology*. They also had to be serving the church, praying for and seeking out lost neighbors and friends, and recruiting two other men or two other couples who they would invest in over the course of the next year. No one could speak on Sunday morning who was not making disciples as a way of life."

One disadvantage of putting together a team, Gorman says, "is if the team isn't very diverse in age, life experiences, perspective, and race. Depending on the team, and in particular the leader, there can be a danger of group think. The members of the team may not feel free to disagree and challenge each other."

Gorman is a huge proponent of team teaching: "First, it keeps us accountable to faithful exegesis of scripture. Second, it is really helpful in having good application that addresses the diversity of the congregation, especially if our team is diverse. Third, it models to the church the way we want them to prayerfully think through the scriptures and how it applies to life individually and in groups."

THE BIG CHALLENGE:

Recall a recent preaching failure. What is a lesson that you can learn from the failure and what are some steps you can take to avoid it or grow from it? Feeling brave? Share the failure with a friend and also identify the personal lesson you learned from going through that experience.

CHAPTER 14

RAISING THE SECURITY LEVEL

People look at me and go, "You must have it made. You have girls. You have a great life." It's not true. I mean you pull the curtain away, and you see I'm just as insecure and neurotic and scared and vulnerable as anybody.

—John Stamos

Ministers as a group are more resistant to annual review and constructive criticism than any other profession of my acquaintance.

—T. David Gordon, *Why Johnny Can't Preach*

Insecurity wants us to keep track of our failures; grace doesn't even write them down.

—Bob Goff

My earliest memories are of both my grandmothers wagging their index fingers at me, saying, "Jimmy, you're going to be the priest in the family." So I wrestled with this sense that God had a calling on my life. Perhaps it was normative. I asked my brother John and my brother Mike, separately, at different times in different places, the same question, "Ever feel like God was calling you to be a priest?" Both of them gave the same answer: "What is wrong with you?"

I remember struggling with God, finally admitting, "I can never stand up and talk for you God... I won't be a priest...Not now...Maybe later?"

So I ran from God. But a series of events interrupted my Jonah-like trek away from God's will. In fifth and sixth grade at our Catholic school, the teachers tried something different in Religion class. They plugged in the first Video Recording Device I ever experienced and played a moving picture rendition of the Gospels of Matthew, Mark, and Luke. Our class watched the Bible acted out. It was mesmerizing and made Religion a tolerable topic.

When I was in high school one of my uncles and one of my aunts each died within a few days of each other. My mother innocently pronounced, "It always happens in threes." That statement clicked a switch inside of me. Without hesitation, I immediately thought and regretfully remarked, "That might be the most ridiculous thing I've ever heard. It actually always happens in ones!" I then began to question if everything my parents, teachers, and even priests said really was true. What is doctrine, and what is tradition or superstition?

A few days later I went to the grocery store and actually bought, among other items, a Bible. Privately I made a commitment to myself that I would read one chapter every night. For the next few years, no matter how tired I was, or how drunk I might have been on a weekend night, I read a chapter in bed.

The Bible seemed to be mostly consistent with what I was hearing and learning at my Catholic Church, school, and home – except the Bible appeared to be much simpler. The gospel couldn't actually be *good news*, could it? It seemed that the truth was as uncomplicated as ABC: Admit I need a Savior; Believe Jesus died and rose for me; Commit to following Him.

Anyway, I continued running. I ended up at UCLA without many options for housing. So I joined the same fraternity (different chapter) that my Dad had been a part of when he was in college. After moving in my belongings that first day, I realized that I had actually joined the drug fraternity on campus.

Over the next few weeks and months I got to see everything the world had to offer – the sex, the drugs, the rock 'n' roll. I remember going to the wild frat parties, physically taking a step back and observing, "We're doing everything our culture says to do and it is all... so...empty!"

A couple fraternity brothers of mine invited me on a retreat with Cru – a para-church Christian organization. I'm not sure why I agreed to go. Perhaps the decadence of the frat house pushed me to do something to shore up my religious roots. We drove up to the mountains of Southern California and I remember praying, "God, you better take care of me this weekend. After all, you and me will be the only Catholics there."

The speaker spoke about the love of God. I'd heard that a million times before, but for the first time it sunk in strategically. "If God really loved me, then what he wants for me is the best thing. So why am I running?"

During one of the down times, one of my frat brothers awkwardly asked me a question. Jesus tells us that the Holy

Spirit will give us the words to say when we're helping others, and that must have been one of those moments, because my friend's inquiry probably seemed bizarre to even him. He clumsily asked, "What happened at the cross?"

That odd question opened my eyes. I suddenly realized that if Jesus actually died for my sins, then why was I so concerned with sin-management? Why was I striving? I was forgiven. I was free. At that moment I prayed a prayer of commitment to Jesus, I stopped running and decided to give my life to God.

The three of us frat boys had gone up the mountain as nominal believers, but we came down the mountain as true brothers. Instantly, God was working.

We quickly saw a good number of our fraternity brothers commit their lives to God. We became the half-drug/half-Christian fraternity at UCLA. It was really awkward and terribly exciting.

I immediately went down to the Newman Center on campus fully willing to devote my life to the priesthood. The leaders there exhibited an amazing and innocent lack of awareness of the Bible. They asked me to lead studies for them the very first day I showed up. Hmmm? I talked and talked with the priests there and became con-

> As I take steps in obedience, he reveals the next steps – often His will is only given to us on a need-to-know basis.

fidently convinced that my calling wasn't to give my life to some religious order. My calling was to give my life to Jesus.

That was one of the first times I experienced how God's vision for me isn't always crystal clear on the front end. As

I take steps in obedience, he reveals the next steps – often His will is only given to us on a need-to-know basis.

I also quickly became aware that my insecurity in speaking for God had been replaced with a clear calling to make Him known.

Jerry Seinfeld joked, "According to most studies, people's number one fear is public speaking. Number two is death. Death is number *two*. Does that sound right? This means to the average person, if you go to a funeral, you're better off in the casket than doing the eulogy."

Why are we so scared to preach? We're insecure. Why are we so reluctant to share speaking opportunities? We're insecure.

Brett decided to take a break from ministry for a season. The stress of dealing with high-drama, high-insecurity leaders had taken a toll. So he stepped down from his associate role and decided to slide into a local church where he'd be anonymous and could sit undisturbed on the sidelines for a while. As Brett walked incognito into the new church's foyer that first mid-week Bible study, someone spotted him and shouted out, "Hey, Pastor Brett, Pastor Brett, what are you doing here?" Brett's cover was blown. That church's Senior Pastor couldn't help but overhear the encounter. Brett locked eyes with the pastor. Immediately Brett felt his distrust and insecurity. "Why is this guy here?" the Senior leader must have thought. "Is he after my job?" So much for a Brett getting a break.

Was Brett being paranoid? Harold Finch proposed, "It's not paranoia if they're really out to get you."

F. Remy Diederich writes, "Insecurity is at the heart of the dark side. Insecurity feeds all kinds of dysfunction. I've seen too many leaders use their leadership to find healing for their insecurity. In their mind, if people will follow them, it will prove to themselves and others that they are valuable. Most leaders would never admit this is their motivation to lead. And honestly, they probably don't see it. But it's there. And it's destructive."[66]

A lady was walking down the street to work when she saw a parrot on a perch in front of a pet store. The parrot said to her, "Hey lady, you are really ugly." The furious lady stormed past the store to her work. On the way home, she saw the same parrot and it said to her, "Hey lady, you are really ugly." She was incredibly angry now. The next day the same parrot again said to her, "Hey lady, you are really ugly." The lady was so upset that she went into the store and warned she would sue the store and kill the bird. The store manager apologized profusely and promised he would make sure the parrot didn't say it again. When the lady walked past the store that day after work the parrot called to her, "Hey lady." She paused and said, "Yes?" The bird said, "You know."

We all know our issues, so we're all insecure. How can we raise our security level?

How can we get past our insecurity?

We can find an answer in the conversion story of the Apostle Paul in the Book of Acts.

---

66 "Insecurity Archives," F. Remy Diederich, accessed November 25, 2018, http://www.readingremy.com/tag/insecurity/.

> But the Lord said, "Go, for Saul is my chosen instrument to take my message to the Gentiles and to kings, as well as to the people of Israel. And I will show him how much he must suffer for my name's sake."
>
> Acts 9:15 (NLT)

Paul's call was to preach to the Gentiles, to kings, and to the people of Israel.

Years later, Paul was arrested in Jerusalem and bound in chains. That is a plight that would trigger anyone's insecurities. Look at how the apostle handled his insecurity:

> "Brothers and esteemed fathers," Paul said, "listen to me as I offer my defense...
>
> "As I was on the road, approaching Damascus about noon, a very bright light from heaven suddenly shone down around me. I fell to the ground and heard a voice saying to me, 'Saul, Saul, why are you persecuting me?'
>
> "'Who are you, lord?' I asked.
>
> "And the voice replied, 'I am Jesus the Nazarene, the one you are persecuting.' The people with me saw the light but didn't understand the voice speaking to me.
>
> "I asked, 'What should I do, Lord?'
>
> "And the Lord told me, 'Get up and go into Damascus, and there you will be told everything you are to do.'
>
> "I was blinded by the intense light and had to be led by the hand to Damascus by my companions.

A man named Ananias lived there. He was a godly man, deeply devoted to the law, and well regarded by all the Jews of Damascus. He came and stood beside me and said, 'Brother Saul, regain your sight.' And that very moment I could see him!

"Then he told me, 'The God of our ancestors has chosen you to know his will and to see the Righteous One and hear him speak. For you are to be his witness, telling everyone what you have seen and heard. What are you waiting for? Get up and be baptized. Have your sins washed away by calling on the name of the Lord.'"

Acts 22:1,6-16 (NLT)

When tempted with insecurity, Paul went back to his call.

A few chapters and a couple years later, Paul was still in prison. The king is called in to hear his case. Again, this situation would evoke insecurity in anyone. Look at Paul's response:

I used to believe that I ought to do everything I could to oppose the very name of Jesus the Nazarene. Indeed, I did just that in Jerusalem. Authorized by the leading priests, I caused many believers there to be sent to prison. And I cast my vote against them when they were condemned to death. Many times I had them punished in the synagogues to get them to curse Jesus. I was so violently opposed to them that I even chased them down in foreign cities.

One day I was on such a mission to Damascus, armed with the authority and commission of the leading priests. About noon, Your Majesty, as I was on the road, a light from heaven brighter than the sun shone down on me and my companions. We all fell down, and I heard a voice saying to me in Aramaic, "Saul, Saul, why are you persecuting me? It is useless for you to fight against my will."

"Who are you, lord?" I asked.

And the Lord replied, "I am Jesus, the one you are persecuting. Now get to your feet! For I have appeared to you to appoint you as my servant and witness. Tell people that you have seen me, and tell them what I will show you in the future. And I will rescue you from both your own people and the Gentiles. Yes, I am sending you to the Gentiles to open their eyes, so they may turn from darkness to light and from the power of Satan to God. Then they will receive forgiveness for their sins and be given a place among God's people, who are set apart by faith in me."

Acts 26:9-18 (NLT)

Paul recalled his call. In the book of Second Corinthians, when Paul was facing opposition from false teachers in the church, when his authority was being diminished by others – a circumstance that arouses insecurity – again he went back to his call.

I will reluctantly tell about visions and revelations from the Lord. I was caught up to the third heaven fourteen years ago. Whether I was in my body or out of my body, I don't know – only God knows. Yes, only God knows whether I was in my body or outside my body. But I do know that I was caught up to paradise and heard things so astounding that they cannot be expressed in words, things no human is allowed to tell. That experience is worth boasting about, but I'm not going to do it.

2 Corinthians 12:1-5 (NLT)

How can we deal with insecurity?

1. Recognize who God is.

Paul asked this key question:

Who are you, lord?

Acts 9:5 (NLT)

When we realize who God is, we are on our way to losing our insecurities.

Bernie May was a missionary to Peru for over a decade. His ministry in the Amazon jungle required him to travel to some dangerous places. Another missionary encouraged Bernie to purchase a gun for protection. So May secured one, and he even slept with it in his hammock. The pistol offered him a sense of security.

When Bernie returned to the United States, he decided to get rid of the gun. He went outside to fire the cartridges that had been sitting in the gun for nearly ten years. May pulled the trigger: click, then nothing. He pulled the trigger again and again – click, click, click – but nothing else. Every single shell was bad. Bernie May realized that for a decade he'd had a false confidence in a weapon, when all along it was really God who had protected him.

Larry Crabb describes security this way: "Security – a convinced awareness of being unconditionally and totally loved without needing to change in order to win love. Loved by a love that is freely given, that cannot be earned and therefore cannot be lost."

When we realize we have a God who loves us unconditionally, insecurity tends to fade.

When we recognize who God is we understand who we are.

Early in the primary stages of the 1960 Presidential election, Senator John F. Kennedy told another senator he had dreamed that God had told him he would be the nominee. The other senator said it was strange because he had the same dream and God had told *him* he would be the nominee. The two senators told their story of the matching dreams to a Senatorial colleague, Lyndon Johnson. According to Kennedy, Johnson remarked, "I can't remember tapping either of you for the job.

When we see who God is we realize we are not him.

> This is a trustworthy saying, and everyone should accept it: "Christ Jesus came into the world to save sinners" – and I am the worst of them all.
>
> 1 Timothy 1:15 (NLT)

Paul discovered who God is and that made him less full of ego.

From their book, *Extreme Ownership*, Navy SEALs Jocko Willink and Leif Babin declare:

> Ego clouds and disrupts everything: the planning process, the ability to take good advice, and the ability to accept constructive criticism. It can even stifle someone's sense of self-preservation. Often, the most difficult ego to deal with is your own.
>
> Everyone has an ego. Ego drives the most successful people in life – in the SEAL Teams, in the military, in the business world. They want to win, to be the best. That is good. But when ego clouds our judgment and prevents us from seeing the world as it is, then ego becomes destructive. When personal agendas become more important than the team and the overarching mission's success, performance suffers and failure ensues.
>
> Many of the disruptive issues that arise within any team can be attributed directly to a problem with ego. Implementing Extreme Ownership requires checking your ego and operating with a high degree of humility. Admitting mistakes, taking ownership, and developing a plan to overcome challenges are integral to any successful team. Ego can prevent a leader from conducting an honest,

When we understand who God is, and that we are not Him, ego subsides, and so does insecurity.

realistic assessment of his or her own performance and the performance of the team.[67]

When we understand who God is, and that we are not Him, ego subsides, and so does insecurity.

2. Recognize what we are supposed to do.

> I asked, "What should I do, Lord?" And the Lord told me, "Get up and go into Damascus, and there you will be told everything you are to do."
>
> Acts 26:10 (NLT)

God called Paul to preach – to the Jews, to the Gentiles, and to kings. And Paul knew he was to "...teach these truths to other trustworthy people who will be able to pass them on to others" (2 Timothy 2:2, NLT).

Mark Batterson discovered, "God is in the resume-building business."

Maybe God has called you to the most prominent ministry position in your town. Maybe he has called you to something else. Maybe you're to preach to kings! Maybe you're the one to preach to a suspected unresponsive group of people way different than you and mostly disliked like the Gentiles were. Or maybe you're just supposed to reach your own people – like the Jews.

John Calvin put it this way, "Nearly all the wisdom which we possess, that is to say, true and sound wisdom,

---

67   Willink and Babin, *Extreme Ownership,* 100.

consists of two parts: the knowledge of God and of ourselves."

St. Augustine once prayed, "Grant, Lord, that I may know myself, that I may know Thee."

Steve Macchia says, "Consider this too: 'Self-awareness is our only defense against self-deception. No matter how you slice it, without clarity in regards to our awareness of self, we will not fully know the true God who created us in the first place. And, discovering the truth about ourselves is only possible through the work of the Spirit in our lives…and our willingness to prayerfully receive the input of others.'"

> When I recognize God is great and he wants to use even me, I am humbled and ready to go.

In his book *Discover Your Call and Discover Security,* Stu Streeter asks, "Am I doing this because I've been called to it or am I doing this because I am hungry for ambition?"

3. Do the best you can.

College football coach and legend Lou Holz says, "The cure for insecurity is simple: Do the right thing."

John Wooden maintained, "Success is peace of mind which is a direct result of self-satisfaction in knowing you made the effort to become the best of which you are capable."

Did you hear about the guy who stopped going to football games? Every time they huddled up he thought they were talking about him.

Sometimes that guy is me.

I was able to work past my insecurities because God's call on my life to ministry was pretty clear. When I recognize God is great and he wants to use even me, I am humbled and ready to go.

But sometimes the insecurity gets the better of me. I've been able to work through a lot of my issues by meeting with counselors, coaches, trusted friends, and family members. I have a long way to go.

Recently I was shaken by a church planter who insisted he didn't want to work with our network, and he listed a few reasons why. Among other reasons, he claimed we didn't believe in team ministry, and were too denominational – both are spectacularly ridiculous, ill-informed, and misguided claims. For some reason his off-base assumptions affected me more than they should have. He had very little exposure to what we do, I barely knew him, and it took me longer than a minute to shake-off the accusations and move on from him as a recruit I was happy to lose.

My wife said she had a theory, which is code for "I know what is really happening." She pointed out how a deep wound from my childhood had been touched. I was being overlooked, and that poked at my deepest insecurities.

As soon as Lori diagnosed me, I was over the rejection. I understood why I was insecure and moved on. But the incident reminded me that insecurities are real, they are lurking in our lives ready to pounce. I have to continually remember who God is, and what he has called me to do.

Larry Osborne keeps reminding himself and other church leaders: "You have nothing to prove and no one to impress." We simply have to do what God calls us to do.

Dan Southerland says, "Most pastors are too insecure to share the pulpit regularly with a team."

Let's move past our insecurity and embrace the team concept.

MINI-CASE-STUDY
WESTGATE CHURCH, SARATOGA, CALIFORNIA

Lead Pastor Steve Clifford confessed, "I think our team teaching was born out of my own insecurities. When I took the Lead Pastor position at Westgate, I wasn't sure I could carry the load of preaching forty-five to forty-six weeks per year. I had come from a church where one guy was the predominant personality that drove the church and I didn't want this - I didn't think preaching was my primary gift, leadership is. I didn't think I was very good at speaking. So, I told the elders if they wanted me I would only preach thirty weeks per year. It was not a strategic ask, and it was not a courageous ask. It was born out of my own anxieties."

He continues, "The elders went for it. Right away when I started, if you were on staff you were going to preach. This culture means we subconsciously looks for communicators - for almost every position."

Clifford describes himself this way: "I'm like a NFL running back who still has a lot of carries left because I've been sharing the load with others on the team."

Currently Westgate has about fifteen people who preach regularly. Clifford speaks thirty times per year. That leaves twenty-two weeks, with three campuses - that is sixty-six other opportunities per year. With special days and holidays, it became closer to seventy opportunities per year for other team members.

The teaching team meets Thursdays at 10:30am. The church's Worship/Arts Pastor leads the meetings. Each member arrives prepared as if they will be preaching - and the team works three weeks ahead. Clifford concedes, "Collectively it has made me a way better preacher."

The church has learned to develop communicators. They have a deep team. Westgate has been able to plant two campuses as well as other churches. They have created a community where parishioners do not expect God's word to be brought by one person alone. "God's Word gets really amazing when you take a look at it from personalities - introvert/extrovert and male/female. The teaching team concept has brought a real freshness in ministry," says the Lead Pastor. "It is easier at first to do it all by yourself. It's a lot of work to develop people, but more than worth it."

THE BIG CHALLENGE:

Take some extended time to clarify God's call on your life. What is it He is calling you to do? Identify your biggest area of insecurity when it comes to speaking (i.e. looking foolish, being wrong, too small audience, not getting credit, etc.). Confess this to God and ask him to give you the energy, courage, and strength to do what you are called to do.

PART FIVE

WHERE?

CHAPTER 15

FINDING THE OPPORTUNITIES

When opportunity comes, it's too late to prepare.

—John Wooden

If opportunity doesn't knock, build a door.

—Milton Berle

When one door closes, another opens; but we often look so long and so regretfully upon the closed door that we do not see the one which has opened for us.

—Alexander Graham Bell

For the first decade that our Journey Church teaching team was meeting, we tried to work in new speakers with mixed results. Some new teachers fit in swimmingly, but others not so much. We had been together for so long and we had worked through so many preaching materials it seemed overwhelming for a new person to be thrust onto the team and forced to catch up or keep up. We also realized there were a number of other potential teachers in our church.

So we created what we called "Teaching Team Too." We hand-picked some women and men who appeared to have a teaching gift plus a desire to develop. At our first meeting nearly a dozen folks showed up. After the meeting, one of our teaching team regulars privately asked me the obvious question, "What are we going to do with another ten speakers on the team?" "That's a great question," I responded. I didn't have any answers, but I do remember saying something like, "Let's just see what opportunities God gives us."

We've tried to operate with two opportunity philosophies.

Philosophy 1: Preparation comes before opportunity.

Benjamin Disraeli said, "The secret to success in life is for a man to be ready when his time comes."

Abraham Lincoln resolved, "I will prepare and some-day my chance will come."

"What do you have to do to become a doctor?" the six-year-old asked her father. Her dad, seeing an opportunity, said, "You have to do extremely well in school, take a lot of math and science, get into an excellent college, make the highest grades possible, and then go to medical school, and follow that with an internship. Then you can start your own practice. Honey, as smart as you are, you can be anything you want to be." She gave all this a moment's thought and then asked, "What do you have to do to be queen?"

> God has already moved. It's our move. When we take a step, God reveals His next move.

The movie theater where Discovery Church met proved adequate for the time being, but we knew it was not a long-term solution to the church's facility needs. So we embarked on a giving campaign we called, "Time to Start."

It was not time to buy, or time to build, or even time to become dissatisfied with our present meeting place. But it was time to start preparing.

Our giving emphasis peaked on the Sunday before Thanksgiving when we asked folks to bring their extra offerings and pledges. On the Sunday after Thanksgiving we announced the results. The promotion was a big hit.

After the announcement several people asked the obvious question, "What do we do now? What are we going to do with this money we just raised?"

The leadership team didn't actually have an answer. We were just trying to get through the campaign. We simply said, "Hey, let's enjoy the holidays and talk about what's next come January."

On the first Monday in January I received a call from a church in the area. They invited me to meet for coffee where they were blunt and to the point: "Our church is in trouble. Will you take over our buildings, our payments, and our people?" It turned out the money we raised was a perfect fit for this opportunity.

Here's the principle: God moves, we move, God moves. God has already moved. He has sent His Son for us. It's our move. When we take a step, God reveals His next move.

Opportunity comes from the Latin word *opportunus*. It is a compound word made up of *ob*, meaning toward, and *portus,* meaning port or harbor. The simplest definition is to move toward a port or harbor. When a vessel moves into a harbor it sees the port and sees the opportunities.

Tim Pearring stated, "Intentional preparation creates a fresh awareness for opportunities to use that knowledge and experience. If you build it, they will come."

Philosophy 2: Opportunities abound, we simply must notice them.

Thomas Edison quipped, "Opportunity is missed by most people because it is dressed in overalls and looks like work."

Daniel Nuñez revealed, "We never say, 'There is this need...' We say, 'There is this opportunity...'"

A young preacher was asked by the local funeral director to hold a graveside burial service at a small, local cemetery for someone with no family or friends. The preacher started driving to the event early but quickly got himself lost, making several wrong turns. Eventually, half an hour late, he saw a backhoe and its crew, but the hearse was nowhere in sight. The workmen were off to the side, eating their lunches. The diligent young pastor went to the open grave and found the vault lid already in place. Taking out his prayer book, he read through the service. Feeling guilty because of his tardiness, the young speaker preached a long and passionate sermon, sending the deceased to the great beyond in style. As he was returning to his car, he overheard one of the workmen say: "I've been putting in septic tanks for twenty years, but I've never seen anything like that."

> "Opportunity is missed by most people because it is dressed in overalls and looks like work."

Where do we find opportunities for those on our teaching team to get experience in preaching? Look at the opportunities in the Acts of the Apostles.

Paul was arrested in Jerusalem and a violent scene ensued:

> As Paul reached the stairs, the mob grew so violent the soldiers had to lift him to their shoulders to protect him. And the crowd followed behind, shouting, "Kill him, kill him!"
>
> Acts 19:35-36 (NLT)

Paul is being threatened with death and his response is amazing:

> "Please, let me talk to these people." The commander agreed, so Paul stood on the stairs and motioned to the people to be quiet. Soon a deep silence enveloped the crowd, and he addressed them in their own language, Aramaic.
>
> Acts 19:39-40 (NLT)

Paul turns the riot into an opportunity.

Henry Kaiser observed, "Trouble is only opportunity in work clothes."

A few chapters later, Paul used a court hearing to share his faith:

> The governor then motioned for Paul to speak...
>
> Acts 24:10 (NLT)

That led to more opportunities:

> A few days later Felix came back with his wife, Drusilla, who was Jewish. Sending for Paul, they listened as he told them about faith in Christ Jesus.
> Acts 24:24 (NLT)

A similar episode occurred with Paul in front of Festus, his sister, Bernice, and King Agrippa:

> Agrippa interrupted him. "Do you think you can persuade me to become a Christian so quickly?"
> Acts 26:28 (NLT)

In the middle of a shipwreck we see Paul taking the opportunity to speak:

> So take courage! For I believe God.
> Acts 27:25 (NLT)

Albert Einstein was quoted, "In the middle of difficulty lies opportunity."

When Paul arrived in Rome as a prisoner, he used the intrigue about his chains as an opportunity to preach:

> So a time was set, and on that day a large number of people came to Paul's lodging. He explained and testified about the Kingdom of God and tried to persuade them about Jesus from the Scriptures.
> Acts 28:23 (NLT)

The Book of Acts ends this way:

> For the next two years, Paul lived in Rome at his own expense. He welcomed all who visited him, boldly proclaiming the Kingdom of God and teaching about the Lord Jesus Christ. And no one tried to stop him.
>
> Acts 29:30-31 (NLT)

Paul didn't seem to fret about a lack of opportunity. Instead he used every occasion to preach.

> Yes, we live under constant danger to our lives because we serve the Lord, but this gives us constant opportunities to show forth the power of Jesus Christ.
>
> 2 Corinthians 4:11 (TLB)

Peter did likewise:

> Peter saw his opportunity and addressed the crowd.
>
> Acts 3:12 (NLT)

In our church we've used the following occasions to give our teaching team members teaching opportunities:

First, we have potential team members give a presentation during our actual teaching training times. We've created a somewhat artificial preaching opportunity. We ask speaking students to prepare, come dressed as if they were speaking at an actual service, get up on stage, and give us their best shot. It is daunting to preach to a small group of folks, whose primary task is to give feedback on your message. But it is a great training tool.

Second, our approach has been to ask potential speakers to do five minutes during a Sunday sermon. Or we enlist them to preach one point. The Lead Pastor or an experienced member of the team can open up, do the introduction, set the need, and then have the new person speak for their five minutes. Then the leader can come back up and tie things together, and recover the message if necessary. The five-minute approach gets other people some exposure.

> **Almost every sermon lends itself to having someone add a short testimony, story, interview, or point to the message.**

Honestly, almost every sermon lends itself to having someone add a short testimony, story, interview, or point to the message.

Third, we've used "T" Sundays to train our speakers. I like to rate Sundays or weekends on an A, B, C...grading. "A" Sundays are the *Awesome* days, like Easter, Christmas Sunday, and Christmas Eve, maybe a time or two in the Fall or Spring – those rare, natural high-attendance days. "B" stands for *Better* days. The good Autumn, Spring, or first-of-the-year days when people might be more open to attending church. "C" stands for *Crappy*. Let's face it, there are some down days in ministry – summer, early December – times when church-going isn't the first thing on people's minds. And then "D" stands for *Disaster*. You know the "D" Sundays – Memorial and Labor Day Sundays, the

Sunday after Christmas, the two Sundays sandwiching the 4th of July (I think July 5 is the worst-ever day for church because everybody in our culture is up late the night before celebrating).

A few years ago we made a switch. We changed "D" to "T" for *Training* Sundays. We now use those terrible days to get other people experienced in ministry. So, if only twelve people are coming anyway, let the rookie speak – they will take it seriously, and if it is a disaster, no problem – no one was there to see it!

We didn't have to change the letters. Craig Groeschel pastors the largest church in the United States, Life Church in Oklahoma. He says, "We do what we call, 'Developmental weekends.' Most of our churches have six to seven services, every local pastor is allowed to choose different speakers for their services. So if a campus has eight services, we might pick four speakers – everyone gets two services. At our last one we had around eighty speakers. The church loved it. What was really valuable was before the services they all preached for each other, so they learned to receive feedback, to give feedback. Were any of the eighty speakers ready to preach to all of our churches at one time? Probably not, but they were ready to speak at a service or two."

Fourth, we use other church ministries to train speakers. Our youth service features an onstage speaking part. Our youth pastor likes to work in other speakers fairly regularly, so this is a great step for a budding teacher.

Fifth, we send our speakers to other churches. Offering our team for "pulpit supply" is a wonderful way to help other churches, as well as a key ingredient for giving our team more experience.

> Yes, we live under constant danger to our lives because we serve the Lord, but this gives us constant opportunities to show forth the power of Jesus Christ.
>
> 2 Corinthians 4:11 (TLB)

Sixth, we've stayed open to reproduction.

Our church is committed to reproducing itself, in campuses and by starting other churches. We recognize that part of what we do in our teaching training is leadership development for future expansion.

We try to prepare first and then see the opportunities. But sometimes the opportunity comes first.

> That night Paul had a vision: A man from Macedonia in northern Greece was standing there, pleading with him, "Come over to Macedonia and help us!" So we decided to leave for Macedonia at once, having concluded that God was calling us to preach the Good News there.
>
> Acts 16:9 (NLT)

In his book *Opportunity,* Eben Pagan writes:

> Opportunity ignites desire. Instantly. On a primal level. It co-opts our biological machinery and focuses it on one aim, while also activating potent

forces of motivation. Opportunity, therefore, is the way to "get leverage on yourself." It's the way to motivate yourself to take action and achieve your goals. But it can do far more. Opportunity isn't just about shallow opportunism or about acquiring things you want. It's also about a unique aspect of being human – the need to become the best possible version of yourself.

When you discover an opportunity to live your purpose, to do what you alone can do in this world… to be something more than you thought was possible… everything changes. My wife Annie says, "Opportunity is how God courts you." Something spiritual is happening when you come into contact with your higher potential. If you want to inspire yourself, push yourself, energize yourself, and call on your highest motivation, then put yourself in a constant stream of high-quality opportunities, across the key domains of your life. If you want to call forth the highest version of yourself, build a life of increasingly better opportunity.

The Apostle Paul concurred:

So be careful how you live. Don't live like fools, but like those who are wise. Make the most of every opportunity in these evil days.

Ephesians 5:15-16 (NLT)

MINI-CASE-STUDY:
KENSINGTON COMMUNITY CHURCH, TROY, MICHIGAN

Clint Dupin served as the Lead Pastor of Kensington's Birmingham campus. Clint describes the team teaching philosophy handed down by Church Founder and Lead, Steve Andrews: "Team teaching provides more perspectives and deeper insight. We found that certain individuals had way more insight and personal experiences with certain topics. There were also very practical reasons for a team – more efficient especially when it came to time. Instead of sitting in a room by yourself for ten hours trying to figure out what you were going to talk about, you could generate ideas and begin to lay out points and flow."

The church had two different teams. The first team was made up of eight, with both men and women. The second team was led by the eight. So each leader was responsible for recruiting and training their own teams.

Lead Pastors were encouraged to speak no more than sixty percent of the year.

"It was important to find people with an obvious teaching gift," Dupin says. "One really important aspect we would watch for was whether they were worth following. Did they have the mantel of leadership? Did they know how to cast a vision? We would often start seeing them rise to the surface in smaller settings... like leading a team (small group, serve team, mission trip). We would also develop our current student ministry staff as well."

For training, the church utilizes preaching books by Ken Davis and Andy Stanley. Potential speakers were also asked to try hosting a service or greeting the crowd at the beginning. There was practical training as well. "We would carve out two-hour training times during the week and let each of them speak for ten to fifteen minutes and let the team critique and encourage them."

Clint touts the advantages of team teaching as, "Diversity, well rounded, fights against the rock star mentality, rest, more gifts displayed, different personality types celebrated, and topic-communicator fit - certain people are way more experienced speaking on a certain topic."

There can be a downside, Dupin admits: "Too many voices, hurt feelings, putting someone up that doesn't have the gift or isn't ready, or not matching a topic with the right person."

THE BIG CHALLENGE:

Assess your current ministry and scan for any areas of potential opportunities to get more people involved in speaking. At this point, don't rule any ideas out. Ask friends in other churches what they are doing for inspiration.

CHAPTER 16

DON'T MISS MALTA

Most pastoral work takes place in obscurity, deciphering grace in the shadows, blowing on the embers of a hard-used life.

—Eugene Peterson

The best preparation for tomorrow is doing your best today.

—H. Jackson Brown Jr.

I may be going nowhere, but what a ride.

—Shaun Hick

Batting practice just ended, and there was a twenty-minute window before the Independent Western League Solano Steelheads players took infield practice, so I gathered the team in the dugout for a short chapel service. We were delayed in starting because the pregame music blared so loudly over the stadium speakers no one could hold a conversation. I tracked down the kid in charge of the pregame music and asked him kindly if he would turn down the volume so we could conduct chapel. He just stared at me. He didn't actually say anything, but the look on his face communicated, "Hey, I'm the sixteen year old in charge of speaker volume and you're just a chaplain, so I outrank you." After looking at me, he walked away. Frustrated, I asked my friend Gary Wilson, the team's pitching coach and a former major league player, if he could handle the situation. Gary got the music turned off for our benefit. I preached, got in the car, and thought, "I don't need this!" Then I drove home and have never led another baseball chapel service since.

I have preached in many baseball settings: dugouts, clubhouses, luxury boxes, press boxes, parking lots, and even on the field. I've spoken at services in funeral homes, at gravesites, in front yards, backyards, living rooms, dining rooms, bedrooms, and on Neptune Society boats – with and without sea sickness. I've preached at weddings in fields, barns, parks, fire stations, yacht clubs, country clubs, dance halls, banquet rooms, and hotel conference centers. I've spoken at baptisms in lakes, rivers, reservoirs, swimming pools, hot tubs, spas, and oceans – the ocean is louder than I thought!

As a church planter, I've set up stages and spoken in theaters, schools, community centers, open restaurants, closed restaurants, open bars – without an open bar! – and closed bars. I've preached in day care centers, YMCAs, performing arts centers, cafeterias, cafetoriums, gymnasiums, and I have even spoken at all sorts of church buildings. One church plant I led met in a hotel. We used the conference room for the main session, the kids' ministry met in different hotel suites, the junior high met at the pizza joint next door, and the high schoolers met at the steak place across the parking lot.

I've spoken outside under a tree, under a tent, and not under a tent. One time I mentioned it didn't matter to me where I preached – I'd preach on the freeway if they let me. After that talk our set-up team leaders asked if they could speak to me. They confided, "We can get you at least twenty minutes." "What are you talking about?" I responded. "When you said you wanted to speak on the freeway," they continued. "We can block a north and south exit of Highway 99 and set up quickly. We think you'll have twenty minutes." They didn't know I was kidding, and I'm not sure if they were kidding. I've wanted to try that ever since.

I've spoken in most states, several countries, continents, and even in an underground church, which was on the seventh floor in a walkup. My favorite place I have ever spoken was the Hall of Fame room at UCLA!

I'll speak just about anywhere, except maybe the dugout of a minor league ballpark with the music blaring.

I suspect the Apostle Paul had similar mutterings when he ended up off the beaten path.

Paul was planning on speaking in Rome. He had visions of grandeur. Rome was the center of the world in his day, and he was destined to preach there. But a funny thing happened on the way – he was shipwrecked.

A storm raged for fourteen nights, it had to be terrifying.

> Then the sailors bound ropes around the hull of the
> ship to strengthen it.
>
> Acts 27:17 (NLT)

I've held some of my cars together with duct tape, but never held a boat together with rope. Can you imagine? There's more:

The following day they even took some of the ship's gear and threw it overboard.

Acts 27:17 (NLT)

Throwing gear overboard? Can you imagine? But wait, there's more:

So the soldiers cut the ropes to the lifeboat and let it drift away.

Acts 27:31 (NLT)

No more lifeboats? Can you imagine? But wait, it gets even worse:

The crew lightened the ship further by throwing the cargo of wheat overboard.

Acts 27:38 (NLT)

They threw the food overboard! Can you imagine how low the people must have felt after losing everything and the food too? Honestly, sometimes in ministry it feels like we have given our all, we have thrown everything we possess at the problem, yet it still rages on.

They hit a shoal and ran the ship aground too soon. The bow of the ship stuck fast, while the stern was repeatedly smashed by the force of the waves and began to break apart. The soldiers wanted to kill the prisoners to make sure they didn't swim ashore and escape. But the commanding officer wanted to spare Paul, so he didn't let them carry out their plan. Then he ordered all who could swim to jump overboard first and make for land. The others held on to planks or debris from the broken ship. So everyone escaped safely to shore.

Acts 27:41-44 (NLT)

Paul was shipwrecked.

Once we were safe on shore, we learned that we were on the island of Malta...It was cold and rainy... As Paul gathered an armful of sticks and was laying them on the fire, a poisonous snake, driven out by the heat, bit him on the hand.

Acts 28:2-3 (NLT)

Paul's vision was to preach in Rome. Instead he found himself on the tiny, little, cold, rainy, snake-infested island of Malta. Malta is one of the world's smallest islands – it's the smallest national capital in the European Union.

Instead of landing in Rome, Paul ends up on Malta.

Have you ever set out for your idea of Rome and ended up in some tiny, little, cold, rainy, seemingly snake-infested remote spot like Malta? Maybe you feel like you are ministering in Malta right now.

You've wanted to preach in great cathedrals, but you're stuck in a minor league dugout and no one can even hear you.

Before we lament our Maltas, let's finish the story:

Near the shore where we landed was an estate belonging to Publius, the chief official of the island. He welcomed us and treated us kindly for three days.

Acts 28:7 (NLT)

You just might meet some good people on your Malta. Enjoy their kindness.

As it happened, Publius's father was ill with fever and dysentery. Paul went in and prayed for him, and laying his hands on him, he healed him.

Acts 28:8 (NLT)

Maybe your Malta is simply a detour and your job is to heal somebody on the way to Rome. Publius was good to Paul, and Paul was good to Publius. But look what happened next:

Then all the other sick people on the island came and were healed.

Acts 28:9 (NLT)

All the sick people on the island were healed. Now that's a great healthcare plan! Publius-care is the one to vote in. Everybody was healed – everybody!

I like to imagine that Publius – or someone like him – simply cried out to God, "I don't know if you are out there, but please help my father (or son or daughter or friend), they are sick and I am helpless. Please do something God!"

Then the Apostle Paul and his entourage just happen to show up in the unlikeliest of places, and the healing service that erupts proves one hundred percent effective.

Here's the point: *Don't miss your Malta!*

Your present ministry position may not seem like much, but maybe it's a Malta ready for revival.

Where do we find opportunities for teaching team trainees to speak? Anywhere we can! The settings might seem like small potatoes, but God can use the humblest of venues to do the greatest of works.

We can get so enamored with wishing we had the big platform in Rome that we end up missing the major ministry in our Malta. We want so much to be honored in the big leagues we miss the major assignment in a minor place.

Look at the two results in Acts 28:

> As a result we were showered with honors…
>
> Acts 28:10 (NLT)

Why do we want to go to Rome? Is it because we want the big kudos, the great awards, the notoriety, the huge honorarium and the respect? Maybe we are missing the showers of honors that the folks on tiny, rainy Malta are waiting to give us.

Do you want to be showered with honors? That is not necessarily an evil desire.

Paul said this to the Thessalonians:

> So we keep on praying for you, asking our God to enable you to live a life worthy of his call. May he

give you the power to accomplish all the good things your faith prompts you to do. Then the name of our Lord Jesus will be honored because of the way you live, and you will be honored along with him.

2 Thessalonians 1:11-12 (NLT)

It is commendable to try to accomplish all the good things our faith prompts us to do. There is honor in honoring Jesus! But that honor may start in Malta – don't skip your small assignment.

Here is the second result:

As a result we were showered with honors, and when the time came to sail, people supplied us with everything we would need for the trip.

Acts 28:10 (NLT)

The people in Malta gave Paul and his companions *everything* they needed for the trip. The people who yielded their gear, tackle, lifeboats, and food into the sea, were given all of it back and more!

There might be some folks on your little Malta who will end up providing everything you need for your upcoming trip to Rome.

Go ahead and take that small speaking engagement at the rest home or youth group or Sunday School class, or even in the dugout. Maybe that group will give you blessing and support.

Decades ago, I was raising money for a church plant in the Bay Area. I was scheduled to speak at a large men's

> **God will give you all the honors and everything you need for your next trip. Just be faithful in the small jobs.**

retreat but my presentation time was drastically cut because the program ran long. I was bummed as I went out to shoot some hoops on the basketball court during free time. A young man stopped to shoot a few baskets with me for a couple minutes. He asked me a question or two about the church plant and left. That young man tracked down my contact information from somewhere and ended up being an incredible financial supporter.

Around the same time, I spoke at a church in Bakersfield, California. Bakersfield is like Malta without the hype! After services I was invited to lunch at a special restaurant. I followed a convoy of cars across town, nearly thirty minutes on side streets to this so-called hot spot. We pulled into a Furr's Cafeteria. Furr's? Furr's. Furr's is like Denny's without the pizzazz! There was a doctor who came to that lunch. I don't recall meeting him, but he became our top financial supporter for a decade. God reminded me he is the one who provides. Don't miss your Malta! Don't miss your Bakersfield! Don't miss your Furr's Cafeteria!

How does the money part work for teaching teams? Do you pay your teachers? How much? Where do you get the money?

Acts 28 answers all of my money questions. It is a great fundraising chapter because it provides a simple answer: *Don't worry about it!*

God will give you all the honors and everything you need for your next trip. Just be faithful in the small jobs. Your Malta might not be the detour, it might be the destination.

Twice in the last three weeks, scheduled speaking gigs started to go sideways. One saw my scheduled time cut in half. The other event became particularly aggravating as details were constantly changing and my part was minimized. In both cases I just wanted to cancel. Our teaching team met and someone brought up Malta. God was reminding me to remain faithful. Peace overcame me as I traveled out to my Maltas, and both events turned out amazingly better than I could have imagined.

Malta will probably work its way on to your itinerary more times than you plan. Just go with it, God has big plans even in the little places.

I never have spoken at a Baseball Chapel since that minor league incident with the Solano Steelheads in Vacaville, California – I was done. But I do want to report that the minute I got home I made several phone calls. I asked two men from our church if they would finish out the season preaching for me in that Western League. And I set up a new chaplain for the following season. I guess I sensed God leading me to set someone else up to minister in Malta.

MINI-CASE-STUDY:
ONE COMMUNITY CHURCH, LINZ, AUSTRIA

Lead Pastor Ray Schaser recently planted One Community Church with the vision of starting a church planting movement in Linz and beyond. The church began with a teaching team plan.

Schaser says, "Different people represent different demographics, different points of view, and different experiences that can complement each other in preparing for a teaching series or a sermon. I am praying and preparing the basic outline for a sermon series and each individual message. Afterwards I ask our leadership team and launch team members – especially those with teaching gifts – for input."

Pastor Ray implemented a teaching team in his last ministry context. "At the previous church plant (Salem International Church) we had multiple gifted teachers and speakers. We used to sit down at the beginning of the year and map out the teaching schedule. Afterwards I would create an outline and talk people through the expectations and goals for a certain series and the specific message they would preach."

The new church currently has just two teachers. "However, I frequently like to do interviews and testimonies of life change in an interview style, where I prepare together with the person being interviewed and sharing their story," say the pastor.

Where does a new church find potential speakers? Schaser writes, "I have conversations about their theological viewpoints to make sure they convey a biblical and truthful message and holistic perspective of a passage and its context. I ask people about their spiritual gifts and have them speak at a team night before asking them to speak at a Sunday service. I give them feedback to see how they handle it and if they are open for suggestions and ideas to improve in their speaking. I pray about which topics would be a good fit for a certain teacher/speaker."

He continues, "I try to create different platforms and opportunities in small groups, at team gatherings or outreaches to have people speak and be able to evaluate their potential and areas of growth. I assist people I ask to prepare a message in the preparation process and provide input and thoughts on the topic as well as how the message should end and how it is integrated into the service. I ask different people to prepare teachings in different settings to evaluate them before asking them to speak on Sundays."

"The church is built up through the different gifts God has placed in the different speakers and teachers," Schaser explains. "The preparation with a team will always have a more complete view of a certain topic than one single speaker/teacher would on his/her own. The key leader in a church is freed up to lead and not just prepare sermons while he or she is also training others up, helping them develop their God-given potential to teach and communicate his word effectively."

THE BIG CHALLENGE:

Do you have a "Malta" in your life, an opportunity disguised as a dead end? Identify what resources God is providing you through this situation that He could use to make things turn around for His Kingdom. And stop worrying about money. God will give you everything you need.

Consider starting or joining a Preaching Cohort in your region. Contact *www.ExcelNetwork.org/Next-Steps* for more information.

PART SIX

WHEN?

CHAPTER 17

THE WAITING

You usually have to wait for that which is worth waiting for.

—Craig Bruce

Sometimes you have to play a long time to be able to play like yourself.

—Miles Davis

And God said, "Let there be light," and there was light, but the Electricity Board said He would have to wait until Thursday to be connected.

—Spike Milligan

That great theologian, Tom Petty, put it well: "The waiting is the hardest part." Ironically, Petty had to wait for that hit song for him and The Heartbreakers to emerge.

"'The Waiting,' that was a hard one," Petty remembered. "Went on for weeks. I got the chorus right away. And I had that guitar riff, that really good lick. Couldn't get anything else. I had a really hard time. And I knew it was good, and it just went on endlessly. It was one of those where I really worked on it until I was too tired to go any longer. And I'd get right up and start again and spend the whole day to the point where other people in the house would complain. 'You've been playing that lick for hours.' Very hard."

Petty continued, "It's one that has really survived over the years because it's so adaptable to so many situations. I even think of that line from time to time. Because I really don't like waiting. I'm peculiar in that I'm on time, most of the time. I'm very punctual."

"Roger McGuinn swears to me that he told me that line. And maybe he did, but I'm not sure that's where I got it from. I remember getting it from something I read, that Janis Joplin said, 'I love being onstage, and everything else is waiting.' It was about waiting for your dreams and not knowing if they will come true," Petty said. "I always felt it was an optimistic song."

> The longest-lasting stage tends to be deliverance. But the next longest phase is delay. We spend a ton of time waiting.

Tom Petty didn't like waiting. Does *anyone* like waiting?

When I fly to the east coast, I try to schedule my flight with a connection in Chicago's O'Hare International Airport. I always pick the longest line at the grocery store. I go to the gym at 7 p.m. to hit the crowds. I never leave early to beat the traffic. Clearly, I'm kidding.

I'm not a fan of yellow signal lights. My wife chides me for always being in a hurry, "It is not a race," she reminds me. I think, "Those who say it isn't a race are the ones who aren't winning!"

But life is filled with pauses and postponements. Robert Clinton teaches that the stages of faith are:

Dream
Decision
Delay
Difficulty
Dead end
Deliverance

In my experience, the longest-lasting stage tends to be deliverance. That's the good news, but the next longest phase is delay. We spend a ton of time waiting.

The Bible is filled with delays. Abraham and Sarah waited over ninety years to have a baby. The Israelites waited four hundred years in slavery. Moses waited forty years in Midian. God's people waited forty years in the desert. David waited seventeen years after his anointing to fully assume the crown destined to be his. Jeremiah predicted seventy years in exile. Jesus waited thirty years to begin his public ministry.

Ministry appears to be mostly about waiting. I'm not sure I've ever heard a pastor say, "We are growing too fast. God is moving too quickly." Mostly what I hear is, "It's going well, but the growth is not fast enough for me. I'm waiting on God."

"What were you doing when the police arrived?" the judge asked the defendant.

"Waiting, sir."

"For what?"

"For money."

"Who was supposed to give you the money?"

"The man I was waiting for."

"Why was he going to give you money?"

"For waiting."

"Enough of this," exclaimed the judge. "What do you do for a living?"

"I'm a waiter."

We're all waiters, aren't we? When we're waiting for the waiter, aren't we the waiter?"

Perhaps we'd like to start moving toward a teaching team, but we're not ready, we don't have the people, we don't have a plan, so we're waiting.

Jesus told his followers to wait:

> One day Jesus was eating with them. He gave them a command. "Do not leave Jerusalem," he said. "Wait for the gift my Father promised. You have heard me talk about it. John baptized with water. But in a few days you will be baptized with the Holy Spirit."
>
> Acts 1:4-5 (NIV)

Here is the question, what are we supposed to do when we're waiting?

Mandy Hale postulated, "What we are waiting for is not as important as what happens to us while we are waiting. Trust the process."

What we see the apostles do in response to Jesus' call to wait is a list of do's and don'ts for waiters:

1. Don't wait in the wrong line

Recently I was in a "hurry up and wait" mode at O'Hare airport. The airport code is "ORD," which is French for unnecessary delay. Actually, the site was originally a military airport called Orchard Field. Then it was renamed after World War II flying ace, Edward Henry "Butch" O'Hare, in 1949. I believe Butch was an hour late for every meeting in his life. (I had time waiting at the airport to look up the history!) Anyway, my scheduled layover was less than an hour and the trek from gate

Waiting on God makes sense. But some of us wait for everything to be perfect.

to gate took over thirty minutes. When I arrived at my connecting gate, I saw a bunch of folks in line. The airplane was on the ground but waiting for the current plane to push back from the gate. We lingered in line. To our surprise the gate sign suddenly changed to "Springfield." Panic struck. Had we all been waiting in the wrong line for all this time? One passenger summed it up best, "Where is Springfield and who wants to go there?"

Jesus told his followers to wait for the gift of the Holy Spirit. Waiting on God makes sense. But some of us wait for everything to be perfect. Maybe we're waiting for the perfect team member to show up or for one hundred percent of the congregation to get on board.

> King Solomon warned, "If you wait for perfect conditions, you will never get anything done."
>
> Ecclesiastes 11:4 (TLB)

The Cuban cabdriver was leisurely driving us around Havana in his makeshift 1948 Chevy Suburban. He did not seem to have any sense of urgency. Green signal lights in Havana also have a numbered clock – usually starting at 60 – that counts down to zero signaling when the light would turn yellow. We noticed something peculiar about this particular driver. Whenever the clock reached ten seconds or so he would stomp on the brake. We would actually stop at green lights. It was frustrating, but we realized he was having so much fun hanging with our group – and we were paying him extremely well, probably a month's salary in Cuba – that he didn't want the trip to end.

Too many of us get so comfortable we might be stopping at green lights.

2. Don't get too caught up in the calendar

When the apostles met together, they asked Jesus a question: "Lord," they said, "are you going to give the kingdom back to Israel now?" He said to them, "You should not be concerned about times or dates. The Father has set them by his own authority" (Acts 1:6-7, NIrV).

Jesus warned his disciples not to get concerned about times or dates. Yet we get so caught up in the calendar.

"One of the main villains in time management, surprisingly, is the calendar," says behavioral economist Dan Ariely. "The calendar doesn't allow us to write everything on it, so what happens is whatever we can represent on the calendar takes precedence over the things we really want to do."

In our leadership network we encourage leaders to focus on being health driven, not calendar driven.

Solomon was on to it when he penned, "God does everything just right and on time, but people can never completely understand what He's doing" (Ecclesiastes 3:11, GNV).

Gene Simmons put it well when he said, "I don't wait for the calendar to figure out when I should live life."

3. Don't just stand there

Many of us live under the adage: "If good things come to those who wait, why is procrastination so bad?"

Thomas Carlisle observed, "People who would never think of committing suicide or ending their lives think nothing of dribbling their lives away in useless minutes and hours every day."

After Jesus said this to his disciples, he was taken up before their very eyes, and a cloud hid him from their sight.

> They were looking intently up into the sky as he was going, when suddenly two men dressed in white stood beside them. "Men of Galilee," they said, "why do you stand here looking into the sky?"
>
> Acts 1:9-11 (NIV)

Perhaps those two angels were the same ones Luke described in his resurrection account:

> But very early on Sunday morning the women went to the tomb, taking the spices they had pre-pared. They found that the stone had been rolled away from the entrance. So they went in, but they didn't find the body of the Lord Jesus. As they stood there puzzled, two men suddenly appeared to

them, clothed in dazzling robes. The women were terrified and bowed with their faces to the ground. Then the men asked, "Why are you looking among the dead for someone who is alive? He isn't here! He is risen from the dead!"

Luke 24:1-6 (NLT)

The two angels seemed to have one message: Don't just stand there, do something!

A man grows most tired while standing still.

—Chinese Proverb

At a store, a lady stood in line waiting to pay for her items. Three men stood before her in the line. After fifteen minutes she realized that the line wasn't moving at all. She shouted at the cashier, "Is this line going to take all day long?" The cashier replied, "Please step aside ma'am and come here. You are standing behind three mannequins."

If you are not ready to launch a full blown teaching team, you don't have to just stand there, paralyzed from acting.

4. Don't wait alone

They all met together…

Acts 1:14 (NLT)

Waiting is a bit easier if you have someone to wait with. The apostles all waited together.

Maybe you don't have everything in place to launch a teaching team. You could join a teaching team cohort and work on your preaching with others while you wait.

The apostles didn't wait in the wrong line or get caught up in the calendar or just stand there or wait alone. So, what did they do?

1. Pray

> They all joined together constantly in prayer, along with the women and Mary the mother of Jesus, and with his brothers.
>
> Acts 1:14 (NIV)

I suspect God allows times of waiting to push us to him in prayer.

Abraham Lincoln admitted, "I have been driven many times upon my knees by the overwhelming conviction that I had nowhere else to go. My own wisdom and that of all about me seemed insufficient for that day."

E. M. Bounds suggested, "Only God can move mountains, but faith and prayer move God."

While we're waiting for teachers to emerge; for church leaders to embrace a team approach and for team teaching opportunities, let's pray and ask God to provide teachers, move leaders, grant opportunities, and push us forward.

2. Deal with my issues

I've lived through my share of situations where acquaintances, friends, colleagues, and even extended family members turned on me or even moved toward betrayal. But I can't imagine how the eleven apostles felt when they saw Judas turn Jesus over to killers for thirty pieces of silver.

Yet what is almost as amazing is Peter taking the tragedy head on:

> Peter stood up and addressed them. "Brothers," he said, "the Scriptures had to be fulfilled concerning Judas, who guided those who arrested Jesus. This was predicted long ago by the Holy Spirit, speaking through King David. Judas was one of us and shared in the ministry with us."
>
> Acts 1:15-17 (NLT)

While the disciples were waiting for the Holy Spirit to show up, they did some group counseling. They talked about what had happened through their former teammate, Judas.

Maybe God has us in a waiting room because we have some baggage in our past we need to lose.

Did you hear about the guy who was bit by a rabid dog? A friend went to see how he was doing and found the guy writing furiously. The friend told him that rabies could be cured and he didn't have to be worried about a will. The man said, "Will? What will? I'm making a list of the people I'm going to bite!"

Maybe God has us in a waiting room because we have some baggage in our past we need to lose.

Henry Cloud shares in his book *9 Things You Simply Must Do*, "Those who succeed in life cannot ignore their hearts, minds and souls...they listen to what is going on inside, good or bad. They bring it up and deal with it. If it is good, they find a proper place for its expression and growth. If it is not good, they deal with that as well."[68]

> Jesus said, "Father, forgive them, for they do not know what they are doing."
>
> Luke 23:34 (NIV)

Forgiving simply means to let go. When we transition, we need to let go of the past, to let go of the hurt, to let go of the baggage.

> Because of the Lord's great love we are not consumed, for his compassions never fail. They are new every morning. Great is your faithfulness.
>
> Lamentations 3:22-23 (NIV)

God has new compassions for us every morning. Can't we forgive others too?

At the airline check-in, a customer has three bags. He puts them down and says to the clerk, "I'd like you to send this one to Rio, that one to Sydney, and the last one to Cape Town." Her expression clouds, but training takes over and she says, "I'm afraid we can't do that sir." "Why not, you did the last time I flew with you!"

While you are waiting, make sure you get rid of any carry-on bags.

---

68   Henry Cloud, *9 Things You Simply Must Do to Succeed in Love and Life: A Psychologist Probes the Mystery of Why Some Lives Really Work and Others Don't* (Nashville: Thomas Nelson, 2004).

3. Study the Scriptures

Peter continued:

> This was written in the book of Psalms, where it
> says, "Let his home become desolate, with no one
> living in it." It also says, "Let someone else take his
> position."
>
> Acts 1:20 (NLT)

I have got to believe that Pater didn't have Psalm 69 and Psalm 109 memorized. I suspect he came upon those passages when he was reading the Scriptures while he was waiting.

Abraham Lincoln professed, "I am profitably engaged in reading the Bible. Take all of this book that you can by reason and the balance by faith, and you will live and die a better man."

George Washington Carver added, "The secret of my success? It is simple. It is found in the Bible, 'In all thy ways acknowledge Him and He shall direct thy paths.'"

I also believe that God allows seasons of delay to train us. Yellow lights can be a great gift because we can pause and learn and grow before we put the pedal to the metal.

4. Recruit and Replace

> So now we must choose a replacement for Judas
> from among the men who were with us the entire
> time we were traveling with the Lord Jesus.
>
> Acts 1:21 (NLT)

Mike Drury says, "Reproducing requires replacing. If you are going to reproduce regularly, you are going to have to replace repeatedly."

The apostles replaced Judas on the team. And they did this while they were waiting for a green light from God.

We get so excited about recruiting. We gather people on our teaching teams or launch teams or church staffs. But do we ever bother to make sure they are replaced on the team they were on before?

> The waiting might be hard, but it can be a very valuable part of our own development.

Ministry is about constant leadership development. Leadership is always looking for the next person, it is about always recruiting. What about replacing? That is something we can do during the waiting game.

When you are waiting for your teaching philosophy or your preaching team to take shape, spend some time on recruiting and replacing.

Janis Joplin stated, "I love being onstage, and everything else is waiting."

Let's be careful not to adopt that stance. Sure, in putting together a teaching team, in taking that team approach, there will be a lot of waiting. The waiting might be hard, but it can be a very valuable part of our own development.

Tom Petty's conclusion about his song "The Waiting" is telling: "I always felt it was an optimistic song."

While we are waiting for our vision, our team approach to materialize, we can live in anticipation and optimism.

MINI-CASE STUDY:
RESTORE COMMUNITY CHURCH, KANSAS CITY, MISSOURI

Lead Pastor Troy McMahon is a master at developing leaders. One of the church's foundational principles of reproduction is that everyone goes "two deep" – meaning every minister must teach someone else to do what they do. At Restore, it is called *apprenticeship*.

Dan Southerland recently joined the staff at Restore. Dan says, "It is foundational to having a reproduction DNA in your church. I have been using a team teaching approach for thirty years."

He shares, "My belief is that it is healthier for the church, for the pastor, and for the team when we use multiple teachers. If the senior pastor is the only teacher – he is not modeling team, he is not modeling reproduction, he is not teaching someone else to do what he does. The model of leadership that is used in the pulpit is replicated throughout the entire church. Show me a pastor who does all the teaching and I can guarantee you that every team in his church has one leader and that no one else in the church is using team leadership."

At Restore there are four regular speakers, but the church will rotate through four to five more speakers every year. The Lead Pastor speaks fifty percent of the time; two other teachers speak twenty percent each, and the church covers the other ten percent with the once-a-year people.

At Dan's previous church, Westside Family Fellowship in Kansas City, they utilized a 40/30/20 percentage model with the three teachers and covered the other ten percent with the once-a-year people.

Restore's leaders look for gifted communicators who offer a different approach, feel, and style than I offer.

A Thursday run-through of the teaching occurs before the weekend services. The preacher teaches the sermon to eight to ten people, who then give you feedback on what worked, what did not work, what made sense, what did not make sense, and what needs to be changed. This direct feedback approach has been a huge help.

The result of their team approach is the church gets a more balanced offering of teaching.

Southerland contends, "Most speakers are better when they do *not* speak every Sunday. It models team leadership. It takes a lot of work to stay on the same page. Multiple teachers require more preparation and planning – but it is worth it.

THE BIG CHALLENGE:

What are you waiting for right now? Are there any issues in your life that you need to deal with while you are waiting? Pray, read the Scriptures, and confide in godly people – perhaps they can help you identify and deal with anything that needs to be cleared up before you launch the next step of your teaching ministry.

CHAPTER 18

YOU'RE NOT GETTING ANY YOUNGER

Change almost never fails because it's too early. It almost always fails because it is too late.

—Seth Godin

Twenty years from now you will be more disappointed by the things you didn't do than the ones you did do. So throw off the bowlines. Sail away from the safe harbor.

—Mark Twain

Timing isn't the main thing, it's the only thing.

—Miles Davis

"Don't expect to get any reaction from the first service crowd," the pastor warned me as the church staff nodded in agreement. "They are old and unresponsive. But don't worry – the second and third service folks will track with you and hang on every word."

During the first service, I was surprised at the energy-level of the congregation. They laughed at even the worst of my jokes and they stayed glued to every word as I preached. The Associate Pastor ran up to me after the service. "You must be a great comedian," she said excitedly, "because I've never heard that group laugh so much. Nice job!"

I felt pretty good about myself – until the second and third services. My expectations were high, but the folks in those services only laughed a little bit. They were somewhat responsive – nothing like the staff predicted.

Driving home, it hit me. "Uh oh, maybe the older crowd liked me because I am actually…old!"

Here's the point: I am not getting any younger, and neither are you.

When will you start to take team teaching seriously?

I like this Anthony Myers quote: "Not a lot of people know this about me, but I'm a time traveler. The only catch is that so far, I can only travel through time at the same rate everyone else is going."

I suspect a lot of churches travel through time slower than everyone else.

Eric Hoffer suggests, "In times of change, learners inherit the Earth, while the learned find themselves beautifully equipped to deal with a world that no longer exists."

I don't want to lead a church that is beautifully equipped to deal with a world that no longer exists. So I need to know the times.

The children had all been photographed, and the teacher was trying to persuade them each to buy a copy of the group picture. "Just think how nice it will be to look at it when you are all grown up and say, 'There's Jennifer, she's a lawyer,' or 'There's Michael, he's a doctor,' or 'There's Davey, he's the mayor.' A small voice at the back of the room rang out, "And there's the teacher, she's dead."

In *The Laws of Communication for Preaching,* Dave Snyder shares, "D.L. Moody was preaching a service in

Chicago. It was the largest crowd he had ever preached to. He waited to give an altar call until the next service. He figured even more people would turn out the following week. Moody never got to preach that message. Before he could get to the pulpit on Sunday, October 8th, 1871, a cow tipped over a lantern in a barn and started the Great Chicago Fire. The fire burned the city for days. Hundreds died, hundreds of thousands were homeless, and Moody was not able to hold the final service. He vowed from then on he would never hold a service without giving people the opportunity to surrender their lives to Christ."[69]

Is it time to do something different in your preaching, like sharing it with a team?

Will Rogers joked, "Even if you're on the right track, you'll get run over if you just sit there."

Acts chapter twelve outlines the story of Peter's miraculous escape from prison. King Herod had the Apostle John killed, and Peter was next in line.

> The night before Peter was to be placed on trial, he was asleep, fastened with two chains between two soldiers. Others stood guard at the prison gate. Suddenly, there was a bright light in the cell, and an angel of the Lord stood before Peter. The angel struck him on the side to awaken him and said, "Quick! Get up!" And the chains fell off his wrists. Then the angel told him, "Get dressed and put on your sandals." And he did. "Now put on your coat

---

69   Snyder, *The Laws of Communication for Preaching*, Kindle Edition, 56.

and follow me," the angel ordered. So Peter left the cell, following the angel. But all the time he thought it was a vision. He didn't realize it was actually happening. They passed the first and second guard posts and came to the iron gate leading to the city, and this opened for them all by itself. So they passed through and started walking down the street, and then the angel suddenly left him. Peter finally came to his senses. "It's really true!" he said. "The Lord has sent his angel and saved me from Herod and from what the Jewish leaders had planned to do to me!"

Acts 12:6-11 (NLT)

Peter thought he was having a vision, but God had bigger plans.

When he realized this, he went to the home of Mary, the mother of John Mark, where many were gathered for prayer. He knocked at the door in the gate, and a servant girl named Rhoda came to open it. When she recognized Peter's voice, she was so overjoyed that, instead of opening the door, she ran back inside and told everyone, "Peter is standing at the door!"

Acts 12:12-14 (NLT)

Sometimes we're just like Rhoda. We are really excited, but we don't actually take the right action.

"You're out of your mind!" they said. When she insisted, they decided, "It must be his angel."

This is one clear historical and biblical account where the church is clearly wrong. Sometimes well-meaning people are mistaken. Sometimes good people don't have it right. Sometimes church-going folks, even leaders, don't know what they are talking about. These folks were so caught up in their own ways, so stuck in their own heads, and so bound by their own traditions that they thought the idea of something new was ridiculous.

Maurice Maeterlinck warned, "At every crossroads on the path that leads to the future, tradition has placed 10,000 men to guard the past."

> Meanwhile, Peter continued knocking. When they finally opened the door and saw him, they were amazed.
>
> Acts 12:16 (NLT)

Here is the point: *Keep knocking!*

Start now, make something happen. Knock on some doors. Even if they don't open, keep knocking.

> Moses said, "Seventy years are given to us! Some even live to eighty. But even the best years are filled with pain and trouble; soon they disappear, and we fly away…Teach us to realize the brevity of life, so that we may grow in wisdom."
>
> Psalm 90:10, 12 (NLT)

And Paul advised, "You know what sort of times we live in, and so you should live properly. It is time to wake up. You know that the day when we will be saved is nearer now than when we first put our faith in the Lord" (Romans 13:11, NLT).

The Book of Acts recounts:

> Crowds listened intently to Philip because they were eager to hear his message…
>
> Acts 8:6 (NLT)

Philip wasn't the primary pastor. He wasn't on the leadership team. He was simply a recruit to serve people as the church grew. He turned into a great preacher. The crowds were eager to hear him.

You have the same kind of people in your midst. Keep knocking, keep leading, and keep trying to make something happen.

Matt Woodley, editor of *Preaching Today*, admitted, "I can get stuck in my own preaching ruts – my favorite genres of Scripture, my standard outline or typical conclusion, and my consistent way to apply the text. It becomes a Matt Woodley preaching template. For my hearers, this rut gets predicable and maybe even boring. It also prevents me from growing as a preacher. And for our church as a whole it keeps our people from hearing the whole counsel of God."

It is time to step out of our preaching ruts.

Mark Twain said, "Don't put off until tomorrow what can be put off until the day after tomorrow!" He added, "If you're tempted to put something off until tomorrow. Examine it – maybe you can postpone it indefinitely!"

We've been living in postponement mode for way too long.

Alfred Nobel, a Swedish chemist, made his fortune by inventing powerful explosives and licensing the formula to governments to make weapons. In 1888, Nobel's brother died, and a newspaper by accident printed an obituary notice for Alfred instead of the deceased brother.

It identified him as the inventor of dynamite who made a fortune by enabling armies to achieve new levels of mass destruction. Nobel had a unique opportunity to read his own obituary and to see how he would be remembered. He was shocked to think that this was what his life would add up to: he would be remembered as a merchant of death and destruction. Nobel made a huge transition in his life at that time. He took his fortune and used it to establish the awards for accomplishments contributing to life rather than death – the Nobel Prize. And today, Nobel indeed is remembered for his contribution to peace and human achievement, not explosives.

> We are not getting any younger. But we are not dead yet. We can make a difference and we can start now!

We are not getting any younger. But we are not dead yet. We can make a difference and we can start now!

George Patton claimed, "A good plan violently executed now is better than a perfect plan executed next week."

And Shakespeare penned, "Better three hours too soon than a minute too late."

Ray had only heard me speak once when he invited me to preach at his brand new church in Linz, Austria. As we prepped a few minutes before the start of the service, Ray asked, "You know that invitation you gave at the end of the message I heard you preach in Ohio?" "I don't always do that," I confessed. "Can you do that here?" "I don't have to do it," I countered. "I want you to do it, ask people to give their lives to Jesus and have them raise their hands if they commit." "I think it would be better for you to do that, since you are translating," I responded. "I want you to do it," he said. "You're the pastor," you should do it," I answered. Finally, Ray said, "I want to start giving invitations regularly, but it would help me if you did it this first time." I relented.

At the end of the message, with Ray translating, I led the congregation in the ABC prayer: A – Admit we need Jesus. B – Believe Jesus offers us forgiveness based on his death and resurrection for us. C – Commit to following Jesus the best we can for the rest of our lives. Then I asked anyone who prayed that prayer, anyone who made that commitment, to raise their hand and acknowledge it.

Nothing happened. No crickets even chirped. Not a soul raised a hand. I was a bit surprised and more than a tad embarrassed, but I kept talking. I'm not even sure what I said, I just kept talking. I'm not manipulative, so I didn't pretend to see responses or lie, "Yes, I see that hand." I kept talking and thinking, "I told Ray he should have made the invitation." I was working though my insecurities when I

> **Preaching always makes a difference. We might not be able to tell right now, but God is always working.**

remembered the old Campus Crusade adage: "Witnessing is sharing the good news in the power of the Holy Spirit and leaving the results to God."

After what seemed like an eternity, I had calmed myself down and made peace with the lack of response when something odd happened. One young man raised his hand. And then another person raised her hand. And then another, and another, and another and another.

I quickly closed in prayer and sat down. I was disturbed and amazed. The service was over, and I was a still befuddled when Ray rushed up to me to say he was so excited about the response. We were swept away into meetings and I didn't have a moment to process the experience until the next day on the drive back to Germany.

Why didn't anyone respond? And then why did they raise their hands after all that time? Suddenly it hit me – the translation! The delay was for the translating of the message.

Immediately I was reminded about what happens when we preach. Sometimes it seems as if nothing happens. There appears to be no response. We wonder if we are just talking in someone else's sleep. Sometimes the response is immediate. There are times when we can tell we are making a difference.

The truth is, preaching always makes a difference. We might not be able to tell right now, but God is always working. We may be excited about the results or we may never understand the impact, but God is moving through our preaching. So let's keep preaching, and let's encourage others to preach as well.

THE BIG CHALLENGE:

Do something! Ask someone else to preach. Work through a preaching book with a couple folks from your church. Provide another opportunity for budding teachers. Do something, so when someone asks if you read this book, you can answer that you read it, and you can specifically state what action the book led you to take.

For more next steps:

Contact *www.ExcelNetwork.org/Next-Steps*

ACKNOWLEDGMENTS

I want to acknowledge the great support from Journey Church, especially Tim Pearring, Ben Finney, Jeff Sammons, Geoff Wells, Brad Schottle, Scott Jones and Adam Burrell. Sharon Wells was a huge help with editing, encouragement and making things happen.

The Advisory Team of Excel Leadership Network has been extremely encouraging: Luke Allen, David Bennett, Brian Burman, Paul Mints, Karl Roth, Jeff Sharp, Paul Taylor and Geoff Wells.

Willie Nolte and the Transformation Ministries staff have opened the doors for me to meet and serve many pastors.

Thanks to Brett Burner and Lamp Post Publishers; I would not have been able to release this book without him.

A special thank you goes to all of the pastors and churches who participated in the mini-case studies—kudos!

I also want to acknowledge Jim Kennon, David Harris, Eric Beeman and Bryon Scott who were the first to lead teaching team cohorts in their regions.

I'd also like to thank the launch team for *Preaching the Other Way*—Nicci Pearring, Sue Pearring, Gionna Pearring, John Pearring, , Stephen Fussle, Kayleigh Platte, JD Tutell, Dennis Beatty, David Diaso, Todd Toole, Charles Stevens, Clay Monkus, Rick Weber, Stu Streeter,

Ray Schaser, Ace Sligar, Don Gordon, Eric Beeman, Jim Jessup, Steve Bentley, Andy Elliott, Jim Kennon, Ken Hendrix, Kelly Hendrix, Gary Mauro, Scott Jones, Scotty Fountain, Sandy Hope, Nathan Hawkins, Josh Husmann, Bret Johnson, Richard Todd, JT Riley, David Cooke, Brett Dowdy, Bruce Jones, Andy Ziegenfuss, Tom Planck, Jim Dunn, Brian Harrington, Bill Claudio, Clint Dupin, Scott Johnson, Mike Pate, Gregg Svalstad, Matthew Shepherd, Ann Pearring Turley, Gloria Ramos, MP Leek, Aalim Bakari, Nate Thompson, Homer Lewings, Marlan Mincks, Rick McClatchey, Tonya Vroman, Esther Tress, Danny Parmelee, Kory Tedrick, Alex Myose, Seth Kidwell, Nick Villa, Anthony Andrews, Isaac Scott, Dave Lodwig, Jeff Hale, Dan Bergstrom, Andrew Seid, Don Atkins, Roy Peacock, Eric Williams, John Cassidy, Tito Ramirez, Mike Younkman, Tito Ramirez, Oniel Roja, Bob Bixby, Kerrie Schottle, Bradley Crawford, Mike Verlennich, Steve Thurman, Chris Pinion, Colleen Hewitt, Anna Osborne, Omar Limia, David Rosa, Gene Selander, Dana Byers, Dean Degura, Nick Campagna, Daryl McKillian, Jason Hickey, Tonya Reynolds, Eric Gamero, Shane Craven, Rocky Rocholl, Lé Selah, Wayne Deslattes, Preston Adams, Joey Furjanic, Troy McMahon, Tury Nunez, Tom Cullen, Richard Titus, Kenny Stokes, Peyton Jones, Ross Browning, Andrew Alleso, Chris Lewis, Omar Limia, Greg Virtue, Crystal Virtue, Ken Primeau, Matt Van Peursem, Jeff Pallansch, Michelle Pallansch, James Gibson, Cindy Moon, Jason Squires, Joey Szczepaniak, Dillon Barr, Paul Nickerson, Brian Smith Sr., Gary Rohrmayer, and Rachel Prentice.

If you would like more information about teaching team cohorts in your area, or to connect with a coach/consultant on your ministry, please go to:

www.ExcelNetwork.org/Next-Steps